★ THE NEW BIG BOOK OF ★
U.S. PRESIDENTS

BY TODD DAVIS AND MARC FREY

AN IMPRINT OF RUNNING PRESS
PHILADELPHIA • LONDON

9 8 7 6 5 4 3 2 1
Digit on the right indicates the number of this printing

Library of Congress Control Number 2004111135

ISBN 0-7624-2029-4

Cover and interior design by Alicia Freile
Edited by Molly Jay and Elizabeth Encarnacion
Photo research by Jane Sanders and Susan Oyama
Typography: Adobe Garamond, ITC Officina Sans, Univers, and Futura Condensed.

This book may be ordered by mail from the publisher.
But try your bookstore first!

Published by Courage Books, an imprint of
Running Press Book Publishers
125 South Twenty-Second Street
Philadelphia, Pennsylvania 19103-4399

Visit us on the web!
www.runningpress.com

ART CREDITS

Cover credits left to right from top:

John F. Kennedy: © Bernice Schutzer / CORBIS
Abraham Lincoln, Thomas Jefferson and Andrew Jackson: © Bettmann / CORBIS
Franklin Roosevelt: National Portrait Gallery, Smithsonian Institution / Art Resource, NY
George W. Bush: Courtesy of the Office of the Governor, Texas
George Washington, detail, by Gilbert Stuart: Courtesy of the Corcoran Gallery of Art, Washington, D.C., Bequest of Mrs. Benjamin Ogle Tayloe / CORBIS
Theodore Roosevelt: © Bettmann / CORBIS

Interior credits:

AP / Wide World Photos: pp. 36 (top), 38 (bottom), 45 (bottom), 47 (both images), 48 (bottom), 50 (top), 51 (bottom)

National Portrait Gallery, Smithsonian Institution / Art Resource, NY: pp. 20 (bottom), 33 (top), 37, 39 (top), 40, 49, 51 (top), 52

Granger Collection, New York: p. 36 (bottom)

© CORBIS: pp. 44 (bottom), 48

George Washington, detail, by Gilbert Stuart: Courtesy of the Corcoran Gallery of Art, Washington, D.C., Bequest of Mrs. Benjamin Ogle Tayloe / CORBIS: p. 8

© Bettmann / CORBIS: pp. 7, 9, 10, 11 (both images), 12, 13, 14, 15 (both images), 16, 17, 18 (both images), 19, 21 (both images), 22 (all images), 23 (both images), 24, 25, 26, 27, 29, , 30, 31 (all images), 32 (both images), 33 (bottom), 34, 35 (both images), 36 (middle), 38 (bottom), 39 (middle), 42, 43, 44 (top), 45 (middle), 53

© Hulton-Deutsche Collection / CORBIS: p. 41 (both images)

© Bernice Schutzer / CORBIS: p. 45 (top)

© Culver Pictures, Inc.: p. 20 (top)

© 1930 The Detroit News, photo by Milton Brooks: p. 39 (bottom)

© Bill Ross / H. Armstrong Roberts: p. 6

Mike Segar / Reuters / Landov: p. 54 (top)

Courtesy of the Office of the Governor, Texas: p. 54 (bottom)

Painting by Daniel Huntington, 1884, © White House Historical Association: p. 28

Painting by Elizabeth Shoumatoff, © White House Historical Association: p. 46

Painting by Herbert E. Abrams, © White House Historical Association: p. 50

Table of Contents

THE AMERICAN SYSTEM OF GOVERNMENT

THE CONSTITUTION

As the Revolutionary War erupted around them, members of the Continental Congress turned to the difficult task of creating an effective national government. The delegates clashed over whether to form a strong, centralized government or a loosely joined confederation of sovereign states. The resulting Articles of Confederation, ratified in March 1781, represented a compromise. The Articles gave Congress certain powers but reserved significant powers for the states.

The Articles gave each state so much power and independence that the central government had difficulty establishing a national policy. Accordingly, by 1786 many political leaders believed that America needed a stronger national government. Meeting in Philadelphia's Independence Hall, where the Declaration of Independence had been proclaimed a decade before, delegates representing every state except Rhode Island debated the form of that new government. Most delegates agreed that it should be strong without being oppressive, and they worked to balance liberty and order. Ratified in 1788, the Constitution they finally produced represents a series of compromises between national and local authority and between the interests of the large states and the concerns of the smaller ones.

The delegates established a two-house (bicameral) national legislature, with broad powers over commerce, taxation, and war. In the House of Representatives, the lower chamber, representation was based on the total of each state's white population plus three-fifths of its black population. In the Senate, the upper house, each state has two members regardless of its population. The founders expected the House of Representatives to be the branch more responsive to the people. Therefore, congressmen are directly elected by the people and serve two-year terms. The delegates believed that the Senate, in contrast, should be above public whims and passions. Under the original terms of the Constitution, members of the Senate were appointed by state legislatures and served six-year terms. In 1913, the 17th Amendment enabled the people to directly elect their senators.

In addition to Congress, the Constitution created two other equal branches of government: the executive and the judicial. Elected independently of Congress, the chief executive, or President, could originally serve an unlimited number of four-year terms. (In 1951, following Franklin D. Roosevelt's four presidential victories, the 22nd Amendment limited the president to two terms.) The Supreme Court heads the judicial branch. To ensure the judges' independence from political pressure, the Constitution provides that they serve for life.

Checks and Balances

The founders empowered each branch of the government to "check" and "balance" the others, so that no one branch could dominate. For example, the president has veto power over laws enacted by Congress, but his veto can be overridden by a 2/3 vote in both houses. The president also chooses all federal judges, ambassadors, and other heads of government departments (called the cabinet). Most of these appointments have to be approved by the Senate. The Supreme Court also exercises an important brake on the other two branches. Although the Constitution doesn't explicitly give the Court the power to declare a law unconstitutional, the Court began to exercise that power in 1803 and has used it ever since. Finally, Congress can put on trial and remove from office both the president and members of the judiciary.

The Bill of Rights

Despite the checks and balances, the Constitution did very little to protect individual rights. The first ten amendments, adopted in 1791, placed restraints on the power of the federal government over ordinary citizens. They protected individual liberties (such as freedom of speech, the press, and religion), guaranteed trial by jury, and forbade cruel and unusual punishments. These constitutional amendments have protected individuals' basic rights throughout the nation's history.

ELECTING THE PRESIDENT

Presidents have never been elected by the direct vote of the people. Instead, the voters of each state choose a group of men and women—members of the electoral college—who then vote for the president. Each state's number of electors is equal to its total of senators and representatives. California, the most populous state, has 54 electors, while Vermont has only 3. Because of this difference, presidential campaign strategy focuses on larger states like California, New York, Texas, Illinois, Pennsylvania, and Florida. At present, the total number of electors is 538, and a candidate needs a majority of 270 electoral votes to win the presidency. If the candidate doesn't get that number, the House of Representatives decides the election.

The drafters of the Constitution created the electoral college because they wanted to shield the presidential election from direct popular control. According to the electoral procedure originally specified in the Constitution, the electors voted for the two most qualified persons without specifying their choices for president and vice president. The candidate receiving the greatest number of electoral votes would be president, and the second-place finisher would be vice president. In 1804, the 12th Amendment separated the voting for president and vice president.

Aside from a few other minor changes, the procedure worked out by the framers of the Constitution is basically the one in use today. The importance of the presidential electors has changed, however. As political parties developed and vied for power, party interests determined the electors' votes. As a result, the parties presented lists of electors who were pledged to vote for their candidate (although technically an elector may vote as he or she wishes). Electors of a state therefore voted as a unit, and a "winner-take-all" system emerged. Whether a presidential candidate wins a state by one vote or one million votes, he still carries all the electoral votes of that state. In 1824, 1876, 1888, and 2000 the candidate who received the most popular votes ultimately lost the election. Since 1888, the winner of the popular vote has also received the majority of electoral votes.

THE CHANGING ROLE OF THE PRESIDENT

The presidency has an ambiguous place in American politics for two reasons. First, Article II of the Constitution defines the president's role vaguely, allowing presidents and other government officials to argue honestly over what functions the president should and should not perform. The Constitution's imprecise wording allows reasonable people to disagree. Second, the U.S. government is based on a system of checks and balances that forces the government's branches to share power. This balancing is inexact and encourages the executive, legislative, and judicial branches to argue over which governmental office should control particular issues. Fearful of the power of kings, the framers of the Constitution expected this kind of negotiating to occur. They believed that only such negotiations would prevent any one person or group from becoming too powerful and would allow freedom to flourish in the United States.

The presidency's power, then, naturally extends from two different conditions: (1) the personalities of particular presidents, and (2) the demands of individual eras. In short, some presidents become powerful because they are determined to do so, whereas others become powerful because events demand strong presidential action. Andrew Jackson, for example, became a powerful president because he was determined to do so. Believing he understood the will of the American people better than any other government official, he expanded the use of the veto and meddled with the powers of the Supreme Court. Abraham Lincoln, on the other hand, was a powerful president because his era demanded strong leadership. When the United States disintegrated following his election, Lincoln determined that only strong presidential leadership could restore the Union and he acted accordingly. Some politicians opposed Lincoln's powerful actions—the Supreme Court even ruled one of his actions unconstitutional—but he usually managed to overcome his opposition.

Although the presidency was both weak and powerful at different times during the 1700s and 1800s, it became steadily more powerful during the 20th century. Referring to the presidency as a "bully pulpit," Theodore Roosevelt used it to shape public opinion during his years in office, and his success convinced presidents from Woodrow Wilson to Bill Clinton to follow his lead. In addition, America's growing interest in foreign relations during the 20th century gave presidents more chances to "flex their muscles." Because a president serves as commander-in-chief of U.S. military forces, he can operate more independently abroad than he can inside the United States. In fact, many 20th-century presidents have waged war abroad without receiving Congress's permission. American involvement in the Vietnam War, however, convinced many citizens that the presidency had grown too powerful by the 1970s, causing Congress to reassert itself. At the present time, Congress continues to have a very strong voice in American government, and it is unclear how powerful the presidency will be during the 21st century. Only presidents, congressmen, jurists, and voters can decide.

Born: February 22, 1732
Died: December 14, 1799
Birthplace: Pope's Creek, VA
V.P.: John Adams
First Lady: Martha Dandridge Custis

- The only president inaugurated in two cities: New York and Philadelphia
- Wore false teeth made from exotic materials

Slavery

By the 1790s, there were almost 3/4 of a million slaves in the United States. Although the northern states all outlawed slavery between 1777 and 1804, the South became increasingly dependent on slave labor. This dependence increased in 1793 when Eli Whitney invented the cotton gin. This machine simplified the cotton-picking process and saved a tremendous amount of work causing southern cotton production to soar.

GEORGE WASHINGTON

1789–1797

Known as the "Father of his Country," George Washington fully understood the significance of his presidency. While in office, he set the precedents that shaped the job of president. His domestic policies strengthened the national government, and his response to international events helped determine American foreign policy for more than one hundred years.

Washington was born into a well-to-do Virginia planter family. Although he had little formal schooling, he learned the morals, manners, and knowledge necessary for an eighteenth-century Virginia gentleman. Spending much of his time outdoors, he became an excellent horseman and an expert surveyor. Commissioned a lieutenant colonel at the age of 22, Washington fought in the French and Indian War (also known as the Seven Years' War). His exploits and adventures during the conflict between France and Great Britain showed that he had a gift for leadership and made him famous throughout the colonies.

From 1759 until 1775, Washington managed the lands of his Mount Vernon plantation and served in the Virginia House of Burgesses. Devoted to the planter life, he played only a minor role in the initial stages of the American Revolution. Elected to lead the new Continental Army because of his past military experience, Washington held together his ill-trained and poorly supplied troops for six years. Washington's strategy was to harass the more powerful British and avoid major battles. The Continental Army did win some small victories that boosted colonial morale and prevented the Americans' collapse. On Christmas night, 1776, for example, Washington crossed the Delaware River and defeated a surprised British garrison at Trenton, New Jersey. For the next two years, the war swept back and forth across New Jersey and Pennsylvania. As the war in the northern states turned into a deadly stalemate that neither side was able to win, the South became the primary battleground during the final years of fighting. In October 1780, Washington sent Nathaniel Greene to South Carolina. Dividing his army into small, mobile bands, Greene employed what today would be called guerrilla tactics, striking by surprise and then disappearing into the interior. In time, the tide began to turn. Finally, in October 1781, with the aid of French allies, Washington forced the British to surrender at Yorktown, Virginia. After the war, Washington

1744

1756–1763
The British victory in The Seven Years' War decides the future of the North American Continent.

March 5, 1770
At the "Boston Massacre", British soldiers kill five Americans.

1773
The Boston Tea Party ignites the American Revolution.

July 4, 1776
The Declaration of Independence is signed.

1783
The peace treaty with England is signed in Paris, ending The War for Independence.

longed to retire and enjoy the peaceful life of his Mount Vernon fields. The new nation he helped create needed him, however. Probably no other man could have succeeded in welding the states into a lasting union, so he was the unanimous choice for president in 1789.

During his first months in office, Washington enjoyed almost universal support. Within a year, however, there was serious disagreement within Washington's cabinet. Secretary of the Treasury Alexander Hamilton, who had played an important role in securing ratification of the Constitution, favored a strong central government with broad powers. Secretary of State Thomas Jefferson, author of the Declaration of Independence, feared that a strong government might abuse its power and oppress the people. Washington usually took Hamilton's side in these disagreements. The Hamilton vs. Jefferson debate about how much power the Constitution gave the federal government has continued to this day.

Despite the split in his cabinet, Washington was unanimously re-elected in 1792. There was some public criticism of his policies, however. The farmers of western Pennsylvania, for example, protested a government tax on whiskey. Alarmed that the protests might spread, Washington led a federal army against the protesters and quickly restored order. Although the Whiskey Rebellion never really threatened the government, Washington's actions proved that the federal government had the power to enforce its laws.

As president, Washington was much less willing to use military force abroad. When the French Revolution led to a war between France and England in 1793, the president faced a number of diplomatic and domestic problems. The war also divided Washington's cabinet again. This time, Washington refused the advice of both the pro-British Hamilton and the pro-French Jefferson. Instead, knowing the new nation was not prepared to fight, he insisted on neutrality. By the end of his second term, Washington had wearied of politics. To his disappointment, two opposing political parties had developed, centering on the philosophies of Hamilton and Jefferson. Although still very popular, Washington declined a third term, setting an important precedent. In his farewell address, he warned his countrymen about the dangers of political parties and again stressed the importance of neutrality in European affairs.

Washington returned to his beloved Mount Vernon but enjoyed only a short retirement. When he died of a throat infection in 1799, the entire nation mourned him for months.

Native Americans and Blacks in the Revolution

The Revolutionary War involved more than the British and the colonists. It drew in countless Native Americans and slaves as well. Both sides actively sought Indian alliances. Recognizing their immense stake in the outcome, Native American tribes like those in the Iroquois league abandoned neutrality and joined the struggle against the colonists. For blacks, the decision about which side to support was just as difficult. While some blacks sought their freedom by joining the British, nearly 5,000 black patriots, such as Crispus Attucks, bravely fought alongside white colonists.

Women in Revolutionary America

Although the American Revolution was a step forward for political democracy, colonial and revolutionary-era politics did not include women. Although most women did not press for political equality, the more male leaders talked about England's oppressive power, the more American women began to rethink their own domestic situations. The War for Independence encouraged women to write and speak about public events as they raised money for the army and taught their children about the new responsibilities of American citizenship. As a result, women developed new and important connections with public life during these years.

May 25, 1787
The Constitutional Convention in Philadelphia creates the federal government.

1791
The U.S. capital moves from New York City to a site on the Potomac River between Maryland and Virginia.

1791
The Bill of Rights is ratified.

1792
In England, Mary Wollstonecraft publishes *A Vindication of the Rights of Women,* which advances the cause of women's rights.

1797

9

The Virginia and Kentucky Resolutions

To protest the Alien and Sedition Acts, Thomas Jefferson and James Madison wrote the Virginia and Kentucky Resolutions, which argued that the laws were unconstitutional. Jefferson and Madison even insisted that the states had the right to reject federal laws. This nullification argument would become much more important in the years before the Civil War.

Born: October 30, 1735
Died: July 4, 1826
Birthplace: Braintree, MA
V.P.: Thomas Jefferson
First Lady: Abigail Smith

- The first president to live in the White House
- As a lawyer in Boston, he successfully defended the British soldiers accused in the Boston Massacre

Abigail Adams
(1744-1816)

A charming woman who matched her husband in wit and love of books, Abigail Adams was always disappointed in the lack of opportunities she had as a woman. In letters to her husband, she raised issues about women's lack of power in society and in the family and asked him to recognize the sacrifices women made for the country during the Revolution.

JOHN ADAMS
Federalist, 1797–1801

A statesman who played a central role during the Revolution and its aftermath, John Adams had a long and distinguished public career. As president, Adams weathered a bitter political storm springing from an undeclared war with France.

A Harvard-educated lawyer, Adams became one of the first leaders in the American independence movement. He was a tireless member of both Continental Congresses, where he helped draft the Declaration of Independence and proposed the pattern for the American flag. During the Revolutionary War, he served as a diplomat in Europe and helped negotiate the treaty that ended the fighting. After serving as ambassador to England, he became the country's first vice president in 1789. With Washington's retirement, the 1796 presidential election quickly narrowed to a contest between Adams and Thomas Jefferson. Adams narrowly defeated Jefferson, who became vice president. It was the only time in history that the president and vice president were from different political parties.

As soon as Adams took office, he confronted a serious crisis with France. The "XYZ affair," a diplomatic dispute that came to a head after France attempted to bribe American diplomats, outraged the American public. Shouting "Millions for defense, but not one cent for tribute," many demanded war with France. Despite the battles already taking place on the high seas, Adams—aware of America's military weaknesses—resisted declaring war on France. He did lash out at "enemies" at home, however, by supporting the 1798 Alien and Sedition Acts. Designed to quiet criticism of his administration's policies, these laws generated a firestorm of protest. In 1799, Adams dramatically reopened negotiations with France. By year's end, he had secured an agreement ending the conflict (called the Quasi-War) and defusing the political crisis at home.

Although Adams was widely popular during the Quasi-War, he lost much of his popularity during the last year of his presidency. Denied a second term, he enjoyed a peaceful retirement in Massachusetts and renewed his friendship and correspondence with Thomas Jefferson. He died at the age of 91 on the 50th anniversary of the Declaration of Independence.

1797
The U.S.S. *Constitution*—
"Old Ironsides"—is launched.

1799
Napoleon Bonaparte becomes the virtual ruler of France.

April 24, 1800
The Library of Congress is established.

THOMAS JEFFERSON

Democratic-Republican,
1801–1809

Born: April 13, 1743
Died: July 4, 1826
Birthplace: Shadwell, VA
V.P.: Aaron Burr, George Clinton
First Lady: Martha Wayles Skelton

- Played the violin
- His library of approximately 6,000 books was the basis for the Library of Congress

Political theorist, naturalist, architect, philosopher, and statesman, Thomas Jefferson possessed an inquiring mind and wide-ranging interests. As president, Jefferson greatly expanded the size of the United States but also tried to make the central government smaller and less involved in the lives of the people.

Growing up near the mountains of Virginia, Jefferson inherited both wealth and social standing from his parents. As the youngest member of the Continental Congress, Jefferson wrote the Declaration of Independence in 1776. In 1785, he succeeded Benjamin Franklin as American minister to France. Washington then made Jefferson secretary of state, but Jefferson resigned in 1793 because of his differences with Alexander Hamilton. As vice president under John Adams, he led the opposition to many of Adams's policies. In the presidential election of 1800, Jefferson defeated Adams, and control of the government passed for the first time from one political party to another. Jefferson's party and its vision would dominate American politics well into the 19th century.

As president, Jefferson hoped that America would become an open and equal society of independent farmers who needed few laws. He slashed military spending, cut the budget, and reduced the national debt. Despite his belief in small government, Jefferson used his power as chief executive to buy the Louisiana Territory from France in 1803. Riding the popularity he gained from the Louisiana Purchase, Jefferson easily won re-election in 1804. During his second term, Jefferson was increasingly preoccupied with keeping America out of European wars. While at war with each other, both England and France continued to interfere with American shipping. Basing his foreign policy on Washington's principle of avoiding entangling alliances, Jefferson imposed an embargo in 1807, forbidding all American vessels from sailing for foreign ports. The embargo was ineffective and unpopular. Congress repealed the measure in March 1809, three days before Jefferson left office.

After his presidency, Jefferson lived at Monticello, the family home he began to build in 1770. During his later years, he pursued many projects, such as founding the University of Virginia. He died on July 4, 1826, just hours before the death of his great friend and rival John Adams.

Triangular Trade

Although lacking enough support to outlaw slavery altogether, Jefferson did manage to persuade Congress to ban the slave trade in 1808. Tens of thousands of slaves continued to be smuggled into the country. Before 1808, the slave traders had followed the same triangular route for almost two centuries. They carried rum from distilleries in New England to West Africa and traded it for slaves. The slaves, shackled in the holds of the ships, were taken to the West Indies, where they were traded for molasses. The molasses was taken to New England to make rum, completing the triangle.

The Lewis and Clark Expedition

The Louisiana Purchase instantly doubled the nation's size. To explore the new lands, Jefferson dispatched an expedition led by Meriwether Lewis and William Clark. For nearly two-and-a-half years, this intrepid band of explorers made its way across thousands of miles of unmapped terrain. One of the most important members of the team was a 16-year-old Shoshone Indian girl named Sacagawea. Her ability to communicate with other Native American tribes was crucial to the expedition's success.

1800
Noah Webster begins work on a comprehensive dictionary. He didn't publish the complete dictionary, containing more than 70,000 words, until 1828.

1803
In *Marbury v. Madison*, the Supreme Court establishes the principle of judicial review, enabling it to decide whether an act of Congress is constitutional.

August 8, 1807
The *Clermont*, a steamboat engineered by Robert Fulton, makes its way up the Hudson River and begins carrying passengers and freight.

1809

Dolley Madison
(1768-1849)

Known for her charm and intelligence, Dolley Madison was one of the country's most extraordinary first ladies. During the War of 1812, she also proved she could be remarkably cool in a crisis. As the British approached Washington, Dolley packed up the Declaration of Independence, sending it to safety.

Born: March 16, 1751
Died: June 28, 1836
Birthplace: Port Conway, VA
V.P.: George Clinton, Elbridge Gerry
First Lady: Dolley Dandridge Payne Todd

- Stood 5'4" and weighed about 100 pounds
- Used the pseudonym "Publius"

JAMES MADISON
Democratic-Republican, 1809–1817

Before he became president, James Madison made immense contributions both to political theory and to the founding of the American republic. As president, Madison led his country through a second war of independence against England.

Although often ill as a child, Madison's health improved and he attended Princeton University (then called the College of New Jersey), where he studied history, government, and law. Just over five feet tall and barely 100 pounds, Madison worked tirelessly to draft and defend the Constitution and the more effective national government it created. Later, he helped frame the Bill of Rights and served as secretary of state in Jefferson's administration. As Jefferson's hand-picked successor, Madison easily won election in 1808 and re-election in 1812.

When he assumed office, Madison inherited the naval crisis with Great Britain, which was still forcing American seamen into service and seizing American cargo on the high seas. During the first two years of Madison's presidency, a group of young congressmen—known as the "War Hawks"—demanded a more aggressive response to British attacks. Madison resisted these demands for more than a year but finally gave in to the pressure in June 1812 and asked Congress for a declaration of war. Despite the popular enthusiasm whipped up by the War Hawks, America was not prepared to fight. An American invasion of Canada failed miserably, and the British entered Washington in 1814, setting fire to the White House. Although the peace treaty that was finally signed in December 1814 left the issues that caused the conflict unresolved, a few notable naval and military victories convinced Americans that the war had been a success, resulting in an outpouring of nationalist feeling.

Following the two-term precedent established by Washington, Madison left office in 1816. He retired to Montpelier, his Virginia estate, and spent his remaining years as a respected voice on issues, such as slavery, that already threatened to shatter the new Union. He died in 1836, the last of the Founding Fathers.

Native American Relations

Throughout the early decades of the 19th century, the United States kept taking Native American land, either by conquest or deception. Treaties were made and then broken. Some Indian tribes, led by a Shawnee chief named Tecumseh, fought back. On November 7, 1811, in the Battle of Tippecanoe Creek, the U.S. Army led by William Henry Harrison defeated Tecumseh's warriors. Overall, it proved very difficult to reconcile Native American rights with national expansion.

April 25, 1814
British troops burn Washington, including the White House and the Capitol building, which is still under construction.

September 1814
British bombardment of Fort McHenry inspires Francis Scott Key to write The Star-Spangled Banner.

1814
Francis Cabot Lowell opens the first fully mechanized textile factory in Massachusetts, changing the focus of the northern economy from shipping to manufacturing.

1815
The Hartford Convention fails, destroying the Federalist party.

JAMES MONROE

Democratic-Republican, 1817–1825

Born: April 28, 1758
Died: July 4, 1831
Birthplace: Westmoreland County, VA
V.P.: Daniel D. Tompkins
First Lady: Elizabeth Kortright

- Received all but one electoral vote in the election of 1820
- Left the White House in debt

The last leader of the revolutionary generation to be president, James Monroe governed during the "Era of Good Feelings." Although Monroe followed popular nationalist policies, by the end of his second term ugly sectional divisions had appeared within the country.

Monroe dropped out of the College of William and Mary in 1776 to join the Continental Army. Following the war, he served in the Senate, as minister to France (where he helped negotiate the Louisiana Purchase), and as governor of Virginia. In 1811, President Madison appointed him secretary of state. His abilities and experience made him the natural choice for president in 1816. With little opposition, he easily won re-election in 1820.

During Monroe's administrations, the country grew at an amazing rate, and six states were added to the Union. This rapid growth, fueled by the development of roads and canals, reopened the explosive issue of slavery. Since 1789, politicians had tried to keep slavery safely beneath the surface of political life, and in 1819, there were an equal number of slave states and free states. That same year, Missouri applied for admission to the Union as a slave state, threatening to upset the delicate balance. After months of bitter debate between the North and South, Monroe signed the Missouri Compromise, which temporarily resolved the issue. Missouri gained admission as a slave state while Maine came in to the Union as a free state. In addition to maintaining sectional balance, the deal required that all other new states carved from the Louisiana Territory north of the southern boundary of Missouri were to be free states.

In foreign affairs, Monroe, with the help of his secretary of state, John Quincy Adams, fashioned a bold new policy. Responding to the possibility that Spain might try to regain her former Latin American colonies, Monroe warned Europe in 1823 against further colonization of the region and interference in its nations' internal affairs. Although at the time the U.S. did not have the power to enforce the Monroe Doctrine, the policy has guided U.S. actions ever since.

After his second term was over, Monroe went back to his home in Virginia. He died while visiting his daughter in New York in 1831. Like John Adams and Thomas Jefferson, he died on the 4th of July.

American Literature

The most important writers of the early 19th century were James Fenimore Cooper and Washington Irving. Cooper wrote novels about the frontier, including *The Last of the Mohicans*. Irving's famous short stories included "The Legend of Sleepy Hollow" and "Rip Van Winkle."

Native American Alphabet

Beginning in 1809, Cherokee silversmith and warrior Sequoyah started work on a written language for his tribe. By 1821, he had adapted letters from English, Greek, and Hebrew to create the first written Indian language in North America.

1811–1819
The First section of the Cumberland Road, from Cumberland, Maryland, to Wheeling, in then–western Virginia, is built.

1820
American explorer Nathaniel B. Palmer, on a sailing expedition, first sights Antarctica.

1821
Emma Willard founds Troy Female Seminary, the first college-level school for women.

January 1824
Fur trappers find and cross a wide gap in the Rocky Mountains in present-day Wyoming. Called the South Pass, it was later used by thousands of settlers traveling the Oregon Trail.

1825

The American System

In Congress, Henry Clay of Kentucky championed a series of projects designed to improve and update the country's infrastructure—its roads, bridges, and canals. These projects were part of Clay's larger vision, called the "American system", to create a self-sufficient national economy.

Born: July 11, 1767
Died: February 23, 1848
Birthplace: Braintree, MA
V.P.: John C. Calhoun
First Lady: Louisa Catherine Johnson

- Inaugurated when all of the former presidents except for Washington were still alive
- His wife was pregnant 19 times in 22 years

Women's Work

Most early American factories, especially those in New England, relied on young, unmarried women for their workforce. Working 12-hour days for relatively good wages, these factory girls were the first American women to labor outside the home.

JOHN QUINCY ADAMS

Democratic-Republican, 1825–1829

The career of John Quincy Adams, the son of the second president, in many ways paralleled his father's. During John Quincy Adams's presidency, he struggled with political changes—such as increased voter participation—that were ushering in a new era of American democracy.

As a child, Adams watched the Revolutionary War's Battle of Bunker Hill from his family's farm. Working as a secretary for his father in Europe, he became an accomplished diplomat himself. As secretary of state in the Monroe administration, Adams, making the most of America's limited power, arranged with England for joint occupation of Oregon, acquired Florida from Spain, and formulated the Monroe Doctrine.

According to existing political tradition, Adams, as secretary of state, should have been Monroe's natural successor. By the 1824 election, however, a new generation of politicians skilled in the techniques of mass politics had appeared, and there was heated competition for the presidency. When none of the four candidates received an electoral majority, the election, as in 1800, moved into the House of Representatives. There, Adams won the election with the support of Congressman Henry Clay, even though Andrew Jackson had more popular and electoral votes. (Adams then made Clay secretary of state, leading Jackson to call the deal a "corrupt bargain" to steal the election.)

As president, Adams called for a strong federal program of economic development. Unfortunately, his program of road and canal building, standardization of weights and measures, establishment of a national university, and government support for science and the arts quickly fell victim to sectional conflicts and political partisanship. Adams's administration soon floundered, and for the rest of his term, politicians jockeyed for positions in the political realignment that was under way.

Adams's greatest period of public service took place following his defeat in the 1828 election. From 1830 to his death in 1848, "Old Man Eloquent" served in the House of Representatives, where he fought for civil liberties and against slavery.

October 26, 1825
The Erie Canal, linking New York City to the Great Lakes, is completed.

1827
Freedom's Journal is the first anti-slavery journal to be published by African Americans.

July 4, 1828
Work on the Baltimore & Ohio railroad begins.

1828
James Audubon publishes *Birds of America*, which shows more than 1,000 birds in their natural habitats. The Audubon Society grew out of this effort.

ANDREW JACKSON

Democrat, 1829–1837

Born: March 15, 1767
Died: June 8, 1845
Birthplace: Waxhaw, SC
V.P.: John C. Calhoun, Martin Van Buren
First Lady: Rachel Donelson Robards

• Survived first assassination attempt
• Killed a man in a duel

A fiery man with a famous temper, Andrew Jackson believed in a strong central government. During his time in office, he opposed southern sectionalism and financial elitism while favoring westward expansion.

Born into an immigrant farming family, Jackson joined the army at age 13 to fight for American independence. After the Revolutionary War, he studied law and became a respected attorney. In 1796, he was elected to Congress to represent the state of Tennessee and, one year later, became a member of the U.S. Senate.

During the War of 1812, Jackson returned to army life. Earning the nickname "Old Hickory" for being as tough as wood, Jackson led his troops to victory against the British at the Battle of New Orleans. When he led a successful invasion of Spanish-controlled Florida in 1817, Jackson became a national hero and set his sights on the presidency.

Jackson won more votes than any other candidate in the election of 1824, but congressional negotiations prevented him from becoming president. Claiming that he had been the victim of a "corrupt bargain," an outraged Jackson ran for election again in 1828 and won. His frontier upbringing made him the first "common man" to reach the White House.

As president, Jackson supported a strong central government and prevented state officials from nullifying national laws. Preventing nullification was especially difficult for Jackson during his first term because Vice President John C. Calhoun opposed this effort from within the White House. Jackson also ended presidential support of the Bank of the United States, which he believed undermined the central government and neglected the common people. Jackson also encouraged westward expansion and supported the forced removal of several Native American tribes from their traditional homes. Because disease, starvation, and death accompanied Indian removal, Native Americans labeled their journey the "Trail of Tears."

In 1837, Jackson retired to his Tennessee plantation, The Hermitage. He remained an admired elder statesman until his death in 1845.

Davy Crockett (1786–1836)

A legendary hunter, scout, and woodsman, Davy Crockett helped expand America's borders. Crockett fought the Creek Indians under Andrew Jackson in 1813 and 1814, eventually becoming a colonel in the Tennessee state militia. After serving in the Tennessee legislature, he was elected to the U.S. House of Representatives and brought his famous buckskin clothes and coonskin cap to the nation's capital. In 1835, Crockett moved to Texas in order to help its people break away from Mexico. When Mexican leader Antonio Santa Anna raised an army to resist this effort, Crockett went to war and died with nearly 200 others while defending the Alamo mission. Known for his backwoods charm and homespun wisdom, Crockett remains a symbol of frontier self-reliance.

The Whig Party (c. 1834–1856)

The Whig party conceived of the United States as a unified nation rather than as a confederation of states. Whigs attempted to build the roads, canals, and railroads needed to connect America's expanding frontier to urban and agricultural centers. They hoped to alleviate sectional tensions and fortify the economy. Whigs also believed that Andrew Jackson had made the presidency too strong (they called him "King Andy"), and they worked to preserve congressional power. The Whig party declined in the early 1850s because it did not cope with the issue of slavery effectively.

August 28, 1830
First locomotive built in the U.S., Peter Cooper's Tom Thumb runs on the Baltimore & Ohio.

August 22, 1831
Slave preacher Nat Turner organizes the first serious revolt against slavery.

1835
Alexis De Toqueville's *Democracy in America* is published and provides a unique perspective on American culture.

February 23, 1836
Hoping to prevent Texan independence, 4,000 Mexican soldiers kill 176 Texans defending San Antonio's Alamo mission.

1837

The Panic of 1837

Andrew Jackson's economic policies destabilized the nation's economy and created a series of problems that erupted after Martin Van Buren took office. In May 1837, more than 600 American banks failed and caused people across the U.S. to panic. As people lost their jobs and prices for food and rent increased, workers called for government assistance. Van Buren's failure to provide people with direct assistance upset many Americans and even caused workers in New York to riot. In the end, this depression convinced many Americans that the country needed an independent treasury and a more compassionate government.

Born: December 5, 1782
Died: July 24, 1862
Birthplace: Kinderhook, NY
V.P.: Richard M. Johnson
First Lady: Hannah Hoes

- The first president born as a United States citizen
- The eighth president, the eighth vice president, he lived to see the election of eight different presidents from eight different states

Margaret Fuller (1810–1850)

A path-breaking writer and thinker, Fuller was one of the 19th century's most influential women. She worked with Ralph Waldo Emerson, Henry David Thoreau, and Bronson Alcott to develop and explain Transcendentalism, a philosophy that valued self-reliance, individualism, intuition, and the natural world. Fuller wrote for and edited a Transcendentalist journal, *The Dial,* and in 1845, she published *Woman in the Nineteenth Century.* Her book called for more women's rights and inspired the formation of the Seneca Falls Convention in 1848. Fuller later became the first female foreign correspondent when she traveled to Italy and reported on the European revolutions of 1848. In 1850, Fuller, her husband, and their infant son died in a shipwreck while returning to the United States.

MARTIN VAN BUREN
Democrat, 1837–1841

Martin Van Buren was the first president to be born an American citizen rather than a British subject. Andrew Jackson's hand-picked successor, Van Buren planned to fight for the ideas Jackson had championed before an economic depression stalled his presidency.

The son of a tavern keeper and farmer, Van Buren grew up speaking both Dutch and English. After completing his public education at age 14, he clerked at a local law office and began a career in politics. Between 1813 and 1837, Van Buren held a number of state offices in New York before leaving home to serve as secretary of state and vice president. During these years, Van Buren earned the nickname "the Little Magician" for his ability to manipulate fellow politicians. His skilled support of Andrew Jackson's presidential campaigns won him Jackson's lasting admiration and allowed him to pursue the presidency himself. He easily won the election of 1836.

Van Buren's presidency, however, proved unrewarding. Soon after he became president, the American economy plummeted into depression. Convinced that the economy would correct itself, Van Buren did not allow the central government to help suffering citizens and became steadily less popular as a result. Although Andrew Jackson's monetary policies—especially his attack on the National Bank—were primarily responsible for this depression, Van Buren's opponents took advantage of his misfortune, labeling him "Martin Van Ruin."

The national debate over slavery also undermined Van Buren's presidency. His decision to oppose the annexation of Texas alienated southern politicians and, even worse, angered his longtime supporter Andrew Jackson. Known for his love of fancy clothes, expensive wine, and rich food, Van Buren was politically and personally vulnerable when he ran for re-election. As a result, he lost the election of 1840 to William Henry Harrison, a man whose military background and common touch gave him mass appeal.

Van Buren retired to his New York estate, Lindenwald, and became a vocal opponent of slavery. In 1848, he waged another unsuccessful presidential campaign as a member of the anti-slavery Free Soil party. He remained an advocate of abolition until his death in 1862.

1837
Samuel F. B. Morse invents the telegraph, a form of electronic communication.

August 31, 1837
Ralph Waldo Emerson delivers his oration "The American Scholar."

November 7, 1837
Elijah Lovejoy, a famous abolitionist, is killed by a pro-slavery mob.

December 4, 1837
The Gag Rule goes into effect preventing congressional debate about slavery.

1838
The Underground Railroad is organized to help slaves escape to the North.

WILLIAM HENRY HARRISON

Whig, March–April 1841

Born: February 9, 1773
Died: April 4, 1841
Birthplace: Charles City County, VA
V.P.: John Tyler
First Lady: Anna Tuthill Symmes

- The first candidate to have a campaign slogan
- Gave the longest inauguration speech of any president (8,445 words)

William Henry Harrison served the shortest presidential term in American history. Becoming president at the advanced age of 68, Harrison developed a severe case of pneumonia shortly after his inauguration and became the first president to die in office.

The young William expected to be an important man because his father had both signed the Declaration of Independence and served as Virginia's governor. Originally intending to become a doctor, Harrison joined the army in 1791 and rose to the rank of captain. In 1798, he left the army to become secretary to the Northwest Territory and, two years later, became governor of the Indiana Territory. As governor, Harrison bribed Native Americans to sell their lands to the U.S. government and handed out whiskey that caused alcoholism to run rampant among Indians. These hostile acts angered the Shawnee chief Tecumseh and brought government soldiers and Native Americans to the brink of war. As a result, Tecumseh and his brother organized a defensive group of Indian tribes designed to resist white westward expansion. In 1811, Harrison successfully attacked Tecumseh's village along the Tippecanoe River, earning fame and the nickname "Old Tippecanoe." He strengthened his reputation even more by defeating the British at the Battle of Thames during the War of 1812.

Like Andrew Jackson, Harrison used his military reputation to advance his political career. He served in the U.S. House of Representatives and the Ohio state senate between 1817 and 1828. In 1840, the Whig party nominated him for president, hoping that his military reputation would help him win the election. Making John Tyler his running mate, Harrison used the catchy slogan "Tippecanoe and Tyler Too" to disguise his aristocratic background and advertise himself as a common frontiersman and self-made man. This tactic was effective and helped him defeat Martin Van Buren by a large majority. He was the first Whig elected president. Forty-eight years later, his grandson Benjamin Harrison became president.

The Temperance Movement

The temperance movement was a crusade to restrict the buying and selling of liquor in the United States. Beginning in the 1820s, this movement involved a number of prominent American men and women who believed alcohol corrupted people and ultimately made them unhappy. Temperance became increasingly popular after the Civil War, as many people joined the Women's Christian Temperance Union and the Anti-Saloon League. In 1900, anti-alcohol zealot Carrie Nation brought fame and controversy to the temperance movement when she destroyed saloon liquor and property with a hatchet. This movement ultimately produced the era of Prohibition.

The Amistad Case

In August 1839, 53 African slaves being transported to Cuba aboard the Spanish ship *Amistad* revolted and killed most of their captors. One of the slaves, Cinque, took command of the ship and ordered the surviving Spaniards to steer it into American waters. Although Spain demanded that the U.S. government return the Africans to Spanish control, American opponents of slavery argued that the Africans should remain free. In March 1841, the U.S. Supreme Court ruled that the Africans should retain their freedom and be allowed to return home. Based on the notion that Africans were human beings who possessed certain rights, this case helped undermine the practice of slavery in America.

1841
Transcendentalists form Brook Farm, a utopian community devoted to cooperative living.

1841
Prussian gunsmith Johann Nikolas Dreyse designs the first breech-loading military rifle.

1841
Scottish surgeon James Baird develops hypnosis.

The Annexation of Texas

After Texas won its independence from Mexico in 1836, its government immediately applied to become a part of the United States. Because Texas allowed slavery and intended to enter the Union as a slave state, abolitionists in the U.S. Congress opposed the annexation of Texas. After years of negotiations, the American government finally agreed to admit Texas to the Union as a slave state just before Tyler left office. Mexico, which had never recognized Texan independence, disputed America's right to annex the territory.

JOHN TYLER
Whig, 1841–1845

John Tyler was the first vice president elevated to the presidency due to the chief executive's death. His enemies, therefore, called him "His Accidency." Unlike Andrew Jackson, Tyler believed state governments should be as strong as the central government.

Born into an aristocratic farming family, Tyler attended the College of William and Mary and studied law. He served in the U.S. House of Representatives between 1816 and 1821 before becoming governor of Virginia. In 1827, Tyler joined the U.S. Senate as a Democrat. Because Tyler opposed the unionist ideas of Andrew Jackson, he left the Democratic party and joined the Whigs. Although his principled political stands angered many Whigs, his ability to win southern votes caused the party to make him its vice presidential nominee in 1840.

When President Harrison died, Tyler had to establish his personal authority. Because Tyler had not won election himself, members of Harrison's cabinet believed that he should allow them to lead the country. Tyler refused, establishing the practice that vice presidents could lead the country. As president, Tyler vetoed a congressional attempt to re-create the National Bank that Andrew Jackson had dismantled. This move angered members of the Whig party, causing Whigs to resign from Tyler's cabinet and the party to expel the president from its ranks.

Despite possessing few political allies, Tyler managed to encourage American westward expansion. He used the "Log Cabin" bill to make it easier for settlers to purchase vacant land, and he organized the annexation of Texas. Tyler also worked with Secretary of State Daniel Webster to secure the Webster-Ashburton Treaty, an agreement that settled a dispute with Great Britain concerning America's northeastern border. Still, with no major party willing to support him, Tyler retired from office in 1845 without seeking re-election.

When the Civil War began in 1861, Tyler attempted to negotiate a peaceful settlement between the North and the South. After these negotiations failed, he joined the Confederate government. He died while serving in the Confederate House of Representatives in 1862.

Born: March 29, 1790
Died: January 18, 1862
Birthplace: Charles City County, VA
V.P.: None
First Lady: Letitia Christian, Julia Gardiner

- First president to remarry after being widowed
- Only president to serve in both the United States and Confederate governments

Frederick Douglass (1817-1895)

Born on a Maryland plantation to Harriet Bailey, a slave, and an unidentified white man, Douglass learned to read and write from his master's wife. In 1838, he escaped from the plantation and traveled to Massachusetts, where he became a vocal opponent of slavery. Within 10 years, Douglass opened his own anti-slavery newspaper, the *North Star*, so that he could denounce slavery publicly. When he published his autobiography, *My Bondage, My Freedom*, in 1855, Douglass became the most recognized and respected African-American abolitionist in the United States. During the Civil War, Douglass advised President Lincoln, urging him to use African-American soldiers and provide them with both equal pay and fair promotions.

1841

December 1842
Dr. Charles Minnegerode reportedly trims first Christmas tree.

January 1843
Dorothea Lynde Dix becomes a spokesperson for the rights of the insane.

1843
New York City's German Jews form B'nai B'rith, a community organization that becomes increasingly influential over time.

July 3, 1844
American Caleb Cushing negotiates the Treaty of Wang Hiya, the first commercial agreement between the United States and China.

JAMES K. POLK

Democrat, 1845–1849

Born: November 2, 1795
Died: June 15, 1849
Birthplace: Mecklenburg County, NC
V.P.: George M. Dallas
First Lady: Sarah Childress

- Only president to have been Speaker of the House of Representatives
- Acquired the most land for the United States since the Louisiana Purchase

The last of Andrew Jackson's associates to be president, James Polk rose to the presidency promising to work for the common man and to advance westward expansion. Because no one expected him to become a presidential nominee, Polk was the first "dark horse" candidate to win the presidency.

Born on the old American frontier, Polk established himself as a diligent student before graduating from the University of North Carolina in 1818. After graduation, Polk became a lawyer and served in the Tennessee state legislature. He was then elected to the U.S. House of Representatives, serving as speaker of the House between 1835 and 1839. During that time, he supported President Jackson's attack on the Bank of the United States and argued in favor of westward expansion. Polk then left Congress to become governor of Tennessee.

After defeating Whig candidate Lewis Cass in the election of 1844, Polk focused on exciting American nationalism and expanding America's borders. As a result, he provoked war with Mexico in 1846 in spite of the U.S. Army's meager size. Bolstering the regular army's force of 7,500 men with 100,000 volunteers, the president oversaw military operations that capitalized on Mexico's weaknesses. Although soldiers like Robert E. Lee and Ulysses S. Grant used the war to hone the military skills they later applied during the Civil War, other Americans were not so fortunate: 1,700 American soldiers died in action and 11,000 died of disease. The sons of Senators Henry Clay and Daniel Webster were among the casualties. The Mexican War, however, highlighted Polk's strong leadership abilities and allowed the United States to gain control of the land that eventually became the states of California, Nevada, Arizona, Utah, and New Mexico. Polk also established himself as a strong negotiator during this period by convincing Great Britain to surrender peacefully much of the Oregon territory.

His health collapsing toward the end of his first term, Polk did not seek re-election in 1848. Although he might have expanded America's borders in a more peaceful manner, Polk left office knowing that he had achieved most of his goals. The last strong president before the Civil War, Polk died of cholera a few months after retiring to his home in Tennessee.

The Seneca Falls Convention

In July 1848, Elizabeth Cady Stanton and Lucretia Mott organized America's first major women's rights convention at Seneca Falls, New York. Over the course of one week, female and male reformers discussed the many injustices imposed on American women. At the end of the convention, Stanton penned a document declaring that, because all people were equal, women should possess the right to vote. Although women would not win the right to vote for another 70 years, the Seneca Falls Convention provided women with a chance to voice their ideas and helped launch a women's rights movement that continues to thrive in the United States.

Manifest Destiny

In July 1845, John L. O'Sullivan published an article in the *United States Magazine and Democratic Review* that claimed it was America's "manifest destiny" to claim the North American continent for itself. This popular term served as a rallying cry for citizens interested in gaining new land for the United States by annexing Texas, waging war against Mexico, and claiming Native American territories. Those who believed in the idea of "manifest destiny" argued that America's political and religious institutions were uniquely virtuous. The spread of American institutions and culture, therefore, promised to uplift all of humanity.

1845
Starving due to Ireland's Potato Famine, thousands of Irish begin to emigrate to the United States.

1845
Edgar Allan Poe publishes his haunting book *The Raven and Other Poems.*

March 3, 1847
Congress approves the use of adhesive postage stamps.

July 24, 1847
Eager to escape persecution in the East and Midwest, Mormons begin to settle around Utah's Great Salt Lake.

1849

Harriet Tubman (c. 1820–1913)

Harriet Tubman grew up as a slave on a Maryland plantation. In 1849, she escaped from her master and began a 12-year struggle to help other slaves gain their freedom. Although Tubman was illiterate, she was extremely intelligent and became a prominent member of America's Underground Railroad, an informal system in which both black and white Americans moved escaped slaves to safe areas in the North. She helped an estimated 300 slaves gain their freedom before the Civil War.

ZACHARY TAYLOR
Whig, 1849–1850

The first career soldier to become president, Zachary Taylor earned the nickname "Old Rough and Ready" because of his simple and direct manner. His strong patriotism caused him to oppose sectionalism and hold the nation together.

Zachary Taylor grew up on a prosperous Kentucky plantation. He joined the army in 1808 and participated in the War of 1812, before leading U.S. troops against Native American tribes during the next two decades. In 1837, Taylor strengthened his growing reputation by supervising a victory over the Seminoles at Florida's Lake Okechobee.

After rising to the rank of general, Taylor helped provoke war with Mexico and produced impressive American victories at the Battles of Monterrey and Buena Vista. Yet after Taylor became a national hero, President Polk began to consider him a potential political enemy and removed him from the war's front lines as a result.

After the war, the Whig party nominated Taylor for president. Although Taylor did not believe he was qualified to be president, his deep belief in national service caused him to accept the nomination. Running against Democrat Lewis Cass and the Free Soil party's candidate, Martin Van Buren, Taylor took advantage of low voter turnout and won the election.

As president, Taylor had to decide what to do with the land America had taken from Mexico. Although he owned more than 100 slaves, Taylor proved an atypical Southerner, opposing the spread of slavery into America's new territory. When angry Southerners reacted to Taylor's stand by threatening to remove the South from the Union, the President promised to oppose their rebellion with force.

Taylor, however, died before he could resolve America's growing sectional problems. While giving a long speech on July 4, 1850, Taylor consumed foods and liquids susceptible to Asian cholera. His doctors knew little about the disease and were unable to help him. He died five days later. Although people long believed Taylor's enemies poisoned him with arsenic, recent tests indicate that he died of natural causes.

Born: November 24, 1784
Died: July 9, 1850
Birthplace: Orange County, VA
V.P.: Millard Fillmore
First Lady: Margaret Mackall Smith

- The first president not previously elected to any other public office
- Famous for his sloppy appearance

The Gold Rush

In January 1848, a New Jersey mechanic named John Marshal discovered gold while building a sawmill for John Sutter near what is now Sacramento, California. Word of his discovery quickly spread and thousands of Americans risked their lives to cross the continent and win their fortunes. Although many fortune-seekers died along the way, more than 40,000 people had come to California by 1850, and together they unearthed record amounts of gold. Many of these prospectors chose to settle in California, helping to populate the Far West for the first time.

1849

1849
Henry David Thoreau publishes *Civil Disobedience,* a collection of essays showing how to protest against governmental power.

1849
Elizabeth Blackwell becomes the first American woman to earn a medical degree.

1850
Levi Strauss begins to produce blue jeans.

1850
Nathaniel Hawthorne publishes *The Scarlet Letter.*

MILLARD FILLMORE

Whig, 1850–1853

Born: January 7, 1800
Died: March 8, 1874
Birthplace: Cayuga County, NY
V.P.: None
First Lady: Abigail Powers

- His wife established the White House Library
- In retirement, he served as the president of the Buffalo Historical Society

Overshadowed by flamboyant Senators like Henry Clay, John C. Calhoun, and Daniel Webster, Millard Fillmore was a soft-spoken man determined to ease sectional tensions in the United States. He fulfilled the American dream by overcoming childhood poverty to become president.

A farm worker during childhood, Fillmore became a cloth worker's apprentice at the age of 15. He later worked as a schoolteacher and studied law before entering the world of politics. Working for the influential New York politician Thurlow Weed, Fillmore held state office for 8 years before being elected to the U.S. House of Representatives in 1832. Fillmore then lost his attempt to become governor of New York in 1844 but did serve as that state's comptroller.

In 1848, Fillmore became Zachary Taylor's vice president and presided over heated congressional debates concerning slavery. Always a moderate, Fillmore urged Congress to pass the Compromise of 1850, an agreement that admitted California to the Union as a free state, allowed the extension of slavery into southern territories, and helped slave owners to retrieve escaped slaves.

After Fillmore became president, he temporarily improved relations between the North and the South by signing the Compromise of 1850 into law. Looking beyond America's borders, Fillmore sent Commodore Matthew C. Perry to Japan so that the United States could trade with the Japanese and convince them to assist shipwrecked American sailors.

The Whig party did not nominate Fillmore for re-election in 1852, so he returned to New York to practice law. Determined to unite the North and the South, Fillmore again ran for president in 1856 as a member of the Know-Nothing party but lost badly and retired again. During the Civil War, he continued to press for national compromise, denouncing southern secession while refusing to support President Lincoln.

Harriet Beecher Stowe (1811-1896)

Born into a prominent Connecticut family, Harriet Beecher grew up as a minister's daughter and developed strong religious beliefs. When her father moved to Cincinnati in 1832, Harriet visited Kentucky plantations and became a strong opponent of slavery as a result. After marrying Calvin Stowe and raising 6 children, she wrote *Uncle Tom's Cabin* in 1852. Dramatizing the evils of slavery and depicting African Americans as heroic figures, this novel sold more than 1 million copies and strengthened the anti-slavery movement in the United States. In 1856, Stowe wrote her second anti-slavery novel, *Dred, A Tale of the Great Dismal Swamp,* and became an American celebrity.

The Fugitive Slave Act

An element of the Compromise of 1850, the Fugitive Slave Act allowed slave owners to track escaped slaves into the North and return them to the South. Northern abolitionists believed allowing slave owners to reach into areas where slavery was illegal violated the Compromise of 1820 and made it even more difficult for African Americans to gain their freedom. As a result, this piece of legislation dramatically increased sectional tensions in the United States and brought the nation closer to civil war.

1851
Herman Melville publishes *Moby Dick.*

September 18, 1851
Henry J. Raymond edits the first issue of what eventually became the *New York Times.*

1852
Massachusetts passes America's first compulsory school attendance law.

1853

The Kansas-Nebraska Act

The Kansas-Nebraska Act seriously damaged the political party system, one of the last unifying forces in the nation. It destroyed the Whigs and divided the Democrats. It also spurred the creation of two new parties: the anti-slavery Republicans and the anti-immigrant Know-Nothings. Composed of ex-Whigs and Free Soilers, the Republican Party opposed slavery in the territories but would not interfere where it already existed in the South.

Born: November 23, 1804
Died: October 8, 1869
Birthplace: Hillsborough, NH
V.P.: William R. King
First Lady: Jane Means Appleton

- All three of his children died during childhood
- First president to memorize his inaugural address

Railroads

The 1850s were a boom time for railroads in America. During the decade, workers laid more than 21,000 miles of track that opened up the western United States. The power and speed of the "Iron Horse" thrilled Americans, and railroads became the country's first billion-dollar industry.

FRANKLIN PIERCE
Democrat, 1853–1857

A Northerner who was sympathetic to the South, Franklin Pierce's expansionist policies reignited the question of slavery in the territories. By the end of his term, the slavery issue had increased sectional tension significantly.

Pierce came from a prominent New Hampshire family. After some time in New Hampshire politics, where he earned a reputation as an effective speaker, Pierce served in Washington, first as a congressman and then as a senator. In 1846, inspired by the stories of his older brothers who had fought in the War of 1812, Pierce enlisted as a private in the Mexican War. He ended the war as a brigadier general and, although a "dark horse" compromise candidate, won the presidency in 1852.

During Pierce's presidency, the United States tried to add territory to the Republic. The "Young America" expansionist movement—which included the spread of slavery westward across the Plains and south into the Caribbean—greatly influenced Pierce. Although he failed to purchase large parts of Mexico, Pierce did manage to buy a strip of desert along America's southwestern border. The Pierce administration tried to acquire Cuba, a Spanish colony many Americans thought destined to be part of their country. Despite American pressure and the threat of Cuban revolt, Spain refused to sell the island.

Pierce purchased land from Mexico because it lay in the southern path of a proposed transcontinental railroad. Anxious to see a northern route approved instead, Senator Stephen Douglas of Illinois proposed that residents of the Kansas and Nebraska Territories decide the slavery question themselves (a practice known as popular sovereignty). The resulting Kansas-Nebraska Act repealed the old dividing line between free and slave states as set by the Missouri Compromise of 1820.

With the Kansas Territory up for grabs, slave owners and free soilers rushed into the area and vied for control. Violence soon broke out, making Kansas a preview of the Civil War. Although "Bleeding Kansas" was peaceful by 1856, the controversy made the Democrats unwilling to renominate Pierce. He returned to New Hampshire, leaving his successor to face increased sectional fury.

1853

July 8, 1853
Commodore Matthew C. Perry reaches Japan.

March 3, 1855
Congress approves $30,000 to buy Egyptian camels for the American Southwest.

1855
Walt Whitman publishes *Leaves of Grass*, and Frederick Douglass publishes his autobiography, *My Bondage, My Freedom*.

May 1856
South Carolina Congressman Preston Brooks physically attacks Massachusetts senator Charles Sumner, inflaming sectional emotions.

JAMES BUCHANAN

Democrat, 1857–1861

Born: April 23, 1791
Died: June 1, 1868
Birthplace: Cove Gap, PA
V.P.: John C. Breckinridge
First Lady: None

- The only president never to marry
- Because of the Civil War, Buchanan believed he'd be the last president

Relying on constitutional doctrine and legal theories to solve the slavery problem, James Buchanan presided over a polarized nation. Toward the end of his term, he groped in vain for compromise as the nation started down the final road to civil war.

Born into a well-to-do Pennsylvania family, Buchanan graduated from Dickinson College, where he was a gifted debater. In 1819, after his fiancée died, he entered politics, serving in Congress, as President Polk's secretary of state, and as President Pierce's ambassador to Great Britain. During his diplomatic career, he helped write the Ostend Manifesto, a document that urged leaders to acquire Cuba from Spain by negotiation or force. Living in London during the Kansas-Nebraska controversy, he avoided taking sides. Hoping to capitalize on his neutral positioning, the Democrats turned to him as their nominee for president in 1856. In the election that year, Buchanan defeated John C. Fremont, the first candidate of the new Republican party.

Sixty-five at the time of his election to the presidency, Buchanan was a respected elder statesman. Cautious and conservative throughout his public career, Buchanan was ill-equipped to handle the explosive political realities of his time. Two days into his term, the Supreme Court declared slaves property and not citizens. In the same decision, it also ruled that Congress did not have the power to ban slavery in the territories. Endorsed by the president, the Dred Scott decision only heightened sectional tension, as did the continuing troubles in Kansas, which still had both pro-slavery and anti-slavery governments. In October 1859, fanatical abolitionist John Brown's failed attempt to capture a federal arsenal at Harper's Ferry, Virginia and start a slave revolt brought tensions to the breaking point. Hoping for compromise, Buchanan took no forceful action during the last frantic months of his presidency. He denied that the South had the right to secede from the Union but believed the federal government was powerless to prevent it.

In March 1861, after seven states had already left the Union, Buchanan retired to his Pennsylvania home, where he died seven years later.

The Dred Scott Case

In 1846, the slave Dred Scott filed suit in Missouri for his freedom. He argued that his master had taken him into areas where the Missouri Compromise prohibited slavery, and therefore he should be freed. In 1857, the Supreme Court, which had a majority of southern judges, decided that Scott, despite having lived in the North, remained a slave. The implications of this decision went far beyond Scott's personal freedom. Northerners were outraged by the possibility that slavery might be permitted in free states, where it had long been banned.

John Brown (1800-1859)

During his years of scrapping out a living as a tanner in Pennsylvania and Ohio, John Brown became an anti-slavery activist. Fired by religious zeal, Brown and his family killed five men in Kansas in 1856. Brown then spent three years plotting the capture of Harper's Ferry, Virginia. Caught and hanged after his failed attempt to seize the armory, Brown became a martyr in the North, but his actions struck terror in the South.

1856
The Western Union Telegraph Company is established.

May 1857
American William Walker fails in his attempt to legalize slavery in Nicaragua and then become the leader of that country.

1858
Frederick Law Olmstead begins designing Central Park in New York City.

April 1860
Pony Express mail service begins.

February 1861
Jefferson Davis is elected president of the Confederate States of America

1861

Born: February 12, 1809
Died: April 15, 1865
Birthplace: Hardin County, KY
V.P.: Hannibal Hamlin, Andrew Johnson
First Lady: Mary Todd

- The first president born outside of the original thirteen colonies
- At 6'4", the tallest president

The Union Army and African Americans

African Americans offered themselves as soldiers for the Union in 1861 but largely had been turned away. They did serve as cooks, laborers, and carpenters, however. African American leaders like Frederick Douglass pressed for military service. Although black soldiers were led by white officers and received lower pay, fighting in the Union army was an important step toward citizenship and acceptance by a white society. By the war's end, almost 200,000 African Americans had served under the Union flag.

ABRAHAM LINCOLN
Republican, 1861–1865

Abraham Lincoln governed during the greatest crisis in American history. His humanity, eloquence, and determination to save the Union set him apart as one of America's most extraordinary presidents and the central figure of U.S. history.

The son of a Kentucky frontiersman, Lincoln had a humble backwoods childhood. Despite having less than a year of formal education, he became an avid reader and a powerful writer. Before becoming a successful lawyer in Illinois, Lincoln worked as a rail splitter, a ferryboat captain, a clerk, a postmaster, and a soldier in the army. As a member of the Whig party until it collapsed in the 1850s, Lincoln served several terms in the Illinois legislature and one term in the U.S. Congress, where he criticized the Mexican War and supported several anti-slavery initiatives. In 1858, he ran as the Republican candidate for one of Illinois's Senate seats. Although Lincoln lost the election to Stephen Douglas, his performance in the seven well-attended debates earned him national recognition and the 1860 Republican presidential nomination.

In 1860, Lincoln, who was only on the ballot in the North, won the most fateful election in American history with less than 40% of the popular vote. Even before the unusual four-candidate election, southern militants threatened to secede from the Union if Lincoln was elected. In December, with the Republican victory final, South Carolina made good on its threat to secede. By the time Lincoln delivered his inaugural address in March 1861, six other southern states had left the Union and formed the Confederate States of America. On April 12, 1861, Confederate guns fired the first shots of the Civil War at Fort Sumter in the harbor of Charleston, South Carolina.

To subdue the rebellion, Lincoln immediately took several decisive steps without consulting Congress, such as expanding the armed forces and ordering a naval blockade of Confederate ports. With these executive orders, Lincoln showed he was going to be a strong president. Later, because of the emergency situation, he imposed military law on civilians, suppressed newspapers, and seized private property. Lincoln argued that his vast extension of presidential power was temporarily justified because, as president, he was responsible for defending and preserving the Constitution.

From the beginning, Lincoln made it clear that his primary concern in fighting the war was the preservation of the Union, not

July 1861
Matthew Brady begins to photograph Civil War battles. Brady's dramatic photos shock the northern public.

March 8, 1862
Inconclusive battle occurs between 2 ironclad warships, the U.S.S. *Monitor* and the C.S.S. *Virginia*.

August 20, 1862
Newspaper publisher Horace Greeley writes "A Prayer of Twenty Millions," an editorial recommending emancipation, which influences Lincoln.

the abolition of slavery. He gradually and cautiously changed his position, however. Finally, on January 1, 1863, the president—acting in his capacity as commander-in-chief of the armed forces—issued a proclamation freeing all slaves in those states fighting the Union. Though the Emancipation Proclamation did not immediately liberate southern slaves from their masters, it had tremendous symbolic importance. What had started as a war to save the Union became a struggle to free the slaves. To make emancipation official, Lincoln successfully pressed for the passage of the 13th Amendment, which barred slavery from the United States forever.

Because of the revolutionary effects of emancipation, Lincoln knew there was no longer any chance of reconciliation with the South. In addition, by the end of 1863, the war had reached a bloody stalemate, and Lincoln realized that a Union victory required the complete destruction of the Confederacy. Lincoln had problems finding generals who could execute his total-war strategy, however. When the president finally settled in 1864 on Ulysses S. Grant and William T. Sherman, he gave them his full support, although ultimate victory came slowly and produced thousands of Union casualties. In the end, the North's larger population and superior military-industrial resources—along with timely military victories such as Sherman's capture of Atlanta, which ensured Lincoln's re-election in 1864—enabled it to defeat a war-weary South that had never received the foreign aid it needed to win the war.

Overall, Lincoln's leadership went far beyond just directing the war. Lincoln himself became a symbol of the Union, and his public statements—such as the Gettysburg Address and his Second Inaugural—gave eloquent purpose to the conflict. In addition to abolishing slavery, the Civil War ended the debate over the relationship of the states to the federal government. On April 14, 1865, only five days after the Confederate surrender at Appomattox, Virginia, the president attended a play at Ford's Theater in Washington. There, John Wilkes Booth, a southern sympathizer, shot him. Lincoln died the following day. Millions of Americans grieved for the man whose words and actions had redefined a nation.

The Battle of Gettysburg

In the summer of 1863, General Robert E. Lee led the Confederate Army of Northern Virginia into southern Pennsylvania. At Gettysburg on a hot and humid July 1, Lee came face-to-face with a Union army led by General George Meade. During three days of battle, Lee ordered costly assaults against the Union line. On July 3, the bloody failure of Pickett's Charge sealed the Union victory. Coinciding with Grant's victory at Vicksburg in the West, Gettysburg marked the war's military turning point. On November 19, Lincoln traveled to Gettysburg to dedicate the battlefield cemetery. Although just 272 words long, Lincoln's Gettysburg Address rededicated the North to the war effort.

Jefferson Davis
(1808-1889)

A Mississippi planter, Jefferson Davis was the first and only president of the Confederate States of America. Tall and distinguished, Davis grew up in comfortable circumstances, attended Transylvania University and West Point, fought in the Mexican War before his election to the Senate, and served as secretary of war under Franklin Pierce. Throughout his government career, he supported slavery and states' rights. As president of the Confederacy, Davis faced enormous problems. The new nation had to create everything, from a constitution to postage stamps. Ironically, some of the actions Davis took to win the war—such as drafting soldiers—undermined the southern war effort. Because of their belief in states' rights doctrine, many southern governors refused to cooperate with the Confederate government. A month after the Confederacy collapsed, federal troops captured Davis, who had fled the Confederate capital of Richmond disguised as a woman.

June 1, 1863
General Ambrose Burnside orders the suppression of the anti-Lincoln *Chicago Tribune.*

July 13–16, 1863
The New York draft riots express northern discontent with the war.

October 3, 1863
Lincoln proclaims the last Thursday in November to be Thanksgiving Day.

1864
The phrase "In God We Trust" first appears on U.S. coins.

February 17, 1864
The tiny southern submarine *The Hundley* sinks a Union ship before sinking herself.

The 14th and 15th Amendments

Ratified by the states on July 28, 1868, the 14th Amendment reaffirmed state and federal citizenship for the freed slaves and over time has come to mean that state as well as federal power is subject to the Bill of Rights. The 15th Amendment, ratified in 1870, forbade the states from denying any person the vote on grounds of race, color, or previous condition of servitude.

Born: December 29, 1808
Died: July 31, 1875
Birthplace: Raleigh, NC
V.P.: None
First Lady: Eliza McCardle

- He was 17 before he learned to read
- The only former president elected to the U.S. Senate

Seward's Folly

In 1867, Secretary of State William Seward arranged for the United States to buy Alaska from Russia. Many Americans thought Seward was crazy to pay more than $7 million for the huge unexplored territory. Only later would the foresight of Seward's purchase become clear.

ANDREW JOHNSON
Democrat, 1865–1869

Vice president for only 41 days when Lincoln was assassinated, Andrew Johnson faced the enormous task of handling the postwar peace and reuniting the nation. Throughout his term, he fought with Congress over the direction of Reconstruction.

Andrew Johnson grew up in poverty. A self-educated tailor, he made himself into an effective politician and served Tennessee as congressman, governor, and senator. After Lincoln was elected in 1860, Johnson, a Democrat, remained in the Senate when his state seceded. He therefore became a hero in the North, and the Republicans put Johnson on the ticket with Lincoln in 1864 as a gesture of unity.

When Johnson took office in April 1865, the Union was in a state of crisis. Like Lincoln, Johnson supported a lenient Reconstruction policy for the South. Congressional Republicans, in contrast, wanted to punish the seceding states and transform southern society. These "Radical Republicans" passed laws that divided the South into military districts and sent in the army to take command. Radical Republicans were also concerned with the "Black Codes"—a series of measures adopted by southern states to re-establish white dominance by denying the freed slaves such basic rights of citizenship as the right to vote. Because many white Southerners resisted Reconstruction and wanted to restore their old world, the Black Codes were enforced by violent vigilante groups like the Ku Klux Klan. To protect the rights of the former slaves, Congress established the Freedman's Bureau and passed such laws as the Civil Rights Act of 1866.

From 1866 to 1868, Johnson and Congress continued to clash over Reconstruction policies. As the president steadily lost both public and political support, Congress enacted laws restricting his powers. When Johnson purposefully violated one of these laws, the House of Representatives impeached him. Johnson survived his trial in the Senate by one vote, but his presidency was over. Denied renomination, he retired to Tennessee, which returned him to the Senate in 1875. He died a few months later.

1865
Mark Twain publishes *The Celebrated Jumping Frog of Calaveras County*.

May 16, 1866
Congress authorizes a five-cent coin, nicknamed the nickel.

March 1, 1867
Nebraska is the 37th state admitted to the Union.

October 21, 1868
A devastating earthquake strikes San Francisco, causing more than $3 million in damage.

March 15, 1869
The Cincinnati Red Stockings, the first professional baseball team, is founded.

ULYSSES S. GRANT

Republican,

1869–1877

Born: April 27, 1822
Died: July 23, 1885
Birthplace: Point Pleasant, OH
V.P.: Schuyler Colfax, Henry Wilson
First Lady: Julia Boggs Dent

- Mark Twain helped him publish his memoirs
- Received a speeding ticket on his horse

Ulysses S. Grant brought to the presidency little political experience. The qualities that made him a great Civil War general could not be transferred to the political battlefields of Washington. His presidency was ineffective, and his administration was plagued with scandal.

The son of a successful leather tanner, Grant entered West Point when he was seventeen. (A clerical error listed him on the West Point rolls as Ulysses Simpson Grant instead of by his real name, which was Hiram Ulysses Grant. Grant liked his new name and decided to keep it.) After graduating from West Point, Grant served in the Mexican War alongside Robert E. Lee, his future Civil War foe. After resigning from the army in 1854, he worked unsuccessfully at farming, selling firewood, and clerking in his father's leather-goods store.

Soon after the Civil War broke out, Grant enlisted as a colonel in an Illinois regiment. From 1861 to 1863, he commanded volunteer forces and fought several bloody battles that won control of the Mississippi Valley for the Union. In early 1864, Lincoln made Grant commander of all Union armies. Grant then directed his subordinates to drive through the South while his Army of the Potomac slowly defeated Lee's Army of Northern Virginia.

As a Civil War hero, Grant benefited from the votes of former slaves and won a close election in 1868. Once president, he looked to Congress for direction on Reconstruction issues and often seemed bewildered by the political process. His administration also suffered from incompetence and corruption. There is no evidence that Grant himself was involved in any of the scandals, but his poor choice of associates stained his reputation.

Despite his administration's problems, Grant was re-elected by a comfortable margin in 1872. Soon after his inauguration, a financial crisis caused by over-construction of railroads and the collapse of several banks created a terrible depression that lasted for six years. Grant retired in 1876 to take a trip around the world and work on his memoirs. He completed them one week before he died of throat cancer in 1885.

Industrialization

In 1860, America was still a nation of farmers. The Civil War changed that as the need to supply the troops with clothing and equipment sent the northern industrial economy into high gear. When the war ended, the factories just kept going, and by 1875, America had become one of the greatest industrial nations in the world. More and more Americans moved to the cities of the Northeast and the Midwest to find work in the factories. This enormous change in the country's economy had profound effects, both at home and abroad.

The Telephone

Working at night with a mechanic named Thomas Watson, Alexander Graham Bell invented the telephone in March 1876. Although most people considered Bell's invention a joke, several companies soon saw its commercial possibilities.

May 10, 1869
The first transcontinental railroad is completed.

1870
Hiram K. Revels of Mississippi becomes the first African American elected to the Senate.

October 8–11, 1871
The Great Fire of Chicago destroys nearly four square miles of the city.

June 25, 1876
General George Custer and all of his men are killed when they attack Indians led by Sitting Bull and Crazy Horse.

1876
Mark Twain publishes *The Adventures of Tom Sawyer*.

1876
Colorado is admitted to the Union as the "Centennial State."

Sharecropping

The Civil War had devastated the South. Nearly 4 million slaves were on their own, facing the challenges of freedom. Following the war, most southern farms were worked by freed slaves, who did not own the land. Known as sharecroppers, these men and women tilled the land in return for supplies and a share of the crop, generally about half of the yield. The system was inefficient and kept thousands of freed slaves poor and trapped.

Born: October 4, 1822
Died: January 17, 1893
Birthplace: Delaware, OH
V.P.: William A. Wheeler
First Lady: Lucy Ware Webb

- Won several spelling contests as a child
- His wife was the first First Lady to graduate from college (Wesleyan)

P. T. Barnum

As more people moved to towns and cities following the Civil War, popular culture took on new dimensions. For example, traveling circuses became widely popular. Phineas Taylor Barnum was already America's greatest showman when he started his first circus during the early 1870s. In 1881, he teamed up with James A. Bailey to produce a circus he called the "Greatest Show on Earth."

RUTHERFORD B. HAYES
Republican, 1877–1881

An honorable and decent public servant, Rutherford B. Hayes began his term under difficult circumstances. Forced to make a deal with southern Democrats to win the election, he lost his claim to legitimacy and authority.

Hayes, whose father died before he was born, did well in school, graduating from Kenyon College and then Harvard Law School. Joining the Republican party in the mid-1850s, Hayes devoted much of his time to defending runaway slaves. He fought bravely for the Union during the Civil War and was wounded four times. During two terms in Congress and three as governor of Ohio, he made a name for himself as a trustworthy and honest reformer. This reputation made him an attractive candidate to Republicans, who were still suffering from the disgraces of the Grant administration.

The presidential election of 1876, one of the most controversial ever, was marred by fraud on both sides. The early returns pointed to a victory for Hayes's Democratic opponent, Samuel Tilden. The Republicans challenged the results, however, and a special electoral commission declared Hayes the winner by one electoral vote. The Democrats then protested, and Hayes made a deal. In exchange for the presidency, Hayes ordered the last remaining troops out of the South. Known as the Compromise of 1877, this deal ended the era of Reconstruction and cemented the reunion of South and North. As part of the deal, Hayes also agreed to let Southerners handle race relations themselves, initiating a pattern of presidential inaction on the issue not broken until the middle of the 20th century.

As the newly won civil and political rights of blacks quickly crumbled under white Democratic rule in the South, the North suffered from violent railroad strikes and the West saw deadly clashes between Irish Americans and recent Chinese immigrants. Hayes did manage some small successes during his term, including the enactment of limited civil service reform measures. Hayes had always planned to serve only one term as president, and four years in office did not change his mind. In 1881, he returned to his home in Ohio, where he died in 1893.

1877
The Great Railroad Strike paralyzes hundreds of cities and towns.

1879
Terence V. Powderly is elected president of the Knights of Labor, a powerful national union.

1880
Joel Chandler Harris publishes *Uncle Remus: His Songs and His Sayings,* a collection of authentic African-American folk tales.

1877

JAMES A. GARFIELD

Republican, 1881

Born: November 19, 1831
Died: September 19, 1881
Birthplace: Orange, OH
V.P.: Chester A. Arthur
First Lady: Lucretia Rudolph

- Last president born in a log cabin
- Wrote in both Latin and Greek

The only preacher to win the presidency, James Garfield always believed that he was destined for greatness. Rising from childhood poverty, Garfield became a successful educator and congressman before becoming the second president to be killed in office.

James Garfield was born into a poor family living in a log cabin. When he was 18-months old, his father died and left Garfield's mother to raise her children alone. At age 17, Garfield left home to work on a freighter in the Great Lakes and, later, on a canal boat in the Erie Canal. A traveling preacher later inspired Garfield to quit his nautical career and become an ordained minister.

Fearing that he had become "ripe for ruin" during his brief life on the Erie Canal, Garfield sought to improve himself through education. He attended Ohio's Geauga Seminary for two years and completed his formal education at Massachusetts's Williams College. Garfield later became a professor of classics and eventually served as the principal of Ohio's Western Reserve Eclectic Institute.

When the Civil War erupted, Garfield joined the Union Army and became the Union's youngest major general before leaving the army in 1863 to serve in the U.S. Congress, where he served with distinction for 17 years. In Congress, Garfield was a Republican member of the Electoral Commission that allowed Rutherford B. Hayes to become president in 1876. In 1880, the Republican party made Garfield its presidential nominee. A compromise choice, Garfield's nomination depended on his willingness to make Chester A. Arthur his running mate. Many people believed that such political wheeling and dealing degraded the presidency. Nevertheless he won the presidency by defeating fellow Civil War veteran Winfield Scott Hancock. A powerful orator and outspoken opponent of slavery during his years in Congress, Garfield was well prepared for the presidency.

Garfield had hoped to make the presidency stronger than it had been since Lincoln's assassination, but a bitter religious zealot, Charles J. Guiteau, shot him in the back at Washington D.C.'s Baltimore and Potomac railroad station before he had the chance to do much. Suffering terribly for the next two months, Garfield finally died at his wife's side on September 19, 1881. He had been president less than 8 months.

Clara Barton (1821–1912)

Born in Massachusetts, Clara Barton was a schoolteacher early in life but volunteered to help wounded Union soldiers after the Civil War erupted. A skilled and compassionate nurse, Barton's overwhelming kindness caused soldiers to name her the "angel of the battlefield." After the war, Barton lectured in Europe about her wartime experiences and worked with the International Red Cross to help wounded soldiers when the Franco-Prussian War began in 1870. When this war ended, Barton returned to the United States and founded the American Red Cross in May 1881. She served as the organization's president until 1904.

Gunfight at the O.K. Corral

On October 26, 1881, Wyatt Earp, his two brothers, and John "Doc" Holliday clashed with the Clanton gang in Tombstone, Arizona. The two parties had been threatening each other for months, and bullets quickly began to fly after the groups began arguing in the street. After 30 seconds of furious shooting, the battle ended. Billy Clanton and his friends Frank and Tom McLaury lay dead in the street; Morgan and Virgil Earp were badly wounded. Only Wyatt escaped uninjured. The battle erupted because both sides hoped to control the political development of Arizona. Nevertheless, the savagery of the gunfight illustrates how brutal life could be in the Old West.

1880
Joseph Pulitzer becomes owner of the *St. Louis Dispatch,* the first modern newspaper to emphasize scandals.

July 4, 1881
Booker T. Washington founds the Tuskegee Normal and Industrial Institute to teach vocational skills to African Americans.

1881
Helen Hunt Jackson's *A Century of Dishonor* focuses attention on the plight of Native Americans.

1881

The Gilded Age (1865–1900)

The U.S. economy boomed between 1865 and the turn of the century as new industries based on oil, steel, and steam produced massive amounts of new wealth. A great deal of financial and political corruption accompanied the booming economy. Successful industrialists like Andrew Carnegie, John D. Rockefeller, and J. P. Morgan rejected the label robber barrons, claiming that America's financial elite deserved its success. They built massive homes and threw gaudy parties. Because everyday problems seemed to be covered in gold during this era, writer Mark Twain labeled it "the Gilded Age."

Born: October 5, 1829
Died: November 18, 1886
Birthplace: Fairfield, VT
V.P.: None
First Lady: Ellen Lewis Herndon

- Called "Elegant Arthur" for his fashionable clothes
- Passionately protected his private life from the press

Thomas Alva Edison
(1847–1931)

Born in Milan, Ohio, Edison moved to New York at age 21 to work in the financial industry. In New York, Edison made $40,000 by improving the stock ticker and decided to become a full-time inventor. A tireless worker, Edison invented the gramophone, the motion picture, and the electric light bulb during the next 20 years. In 1882, he built a steam-powered station that supplied New York City with electricity. Literally turning darkness into light, Edison changed the course of history.

CHESTER A. ARTHUR
Republican, 1881–1885

Few people expected Chester Arthur to be a good president. Overly fond of money and power, Arthur had stained his reputation by tolerating corruption during his stint as New York City's chief customs officer. Yet Arthur turned over a new leaf after becoming president and worked to reform government.

The son of a traveling minister, Arthur attended a variety of schools during his childhood. He later attended New York's Union College, graduating at age 18. He then became an idealistic lawyer who defended the civil rights of African Americans before serving in the Union Army as a quartermaster general.

After the war, Arthur pursued a career in New York City politics. In 1871, President Ulysses S. Grant appointed him collector of customs for the Port of New York, where he allowed corrupt political and business elites to buy and sell favors. When Arthur refused to cooperate with a federal investigation of the customs house, President Rutherford B. Hayes fired him.

Despite his poor reputation, the Republican party made Arthur its vice presidential candidate in 1880 and allowed him to organize James Garfield's campaign. After Garfield died, Arthur proved his worth by refusing to appoint his corrupt business partners and by helping to reform the U.S. Civil Service. He also attempted to strengthen the U.S. Navy and conserve America's natural resources. By preventing powerful Republican senators like Roscoe Corkling from controlling his presidential actions, Arthur convinced many doubters that he was a good leader and a decent person. Few people had expected him to act so honestly in office.

As time passed, the presidency's long hours and heavy strains depressed Arthur, and he began to avoid difficult tasks. Secretly suffering from a kidney disorder known as Bright's disease, Arthur took long vacations on the presidential yacht and entertained guests with lavish 14-course dinners. Exhausted and in poor health, he decided not to run for re-election in 1884. During the two years before his death in 1886, Arthur became so concerned with concealing his many unethical acts that he burned his public and private papers.

1881

January 2, 1882
John Rockefeller forms Standard Oil Trust, the first modern corporation.

August 18, 1882
Congress allows selective immigration restriction in order to exclude specific groups.

March 24, 1883
Telephone service between New York and Chicago begins.

1884
William Le Baron Jenne builds the first American skyscraper in Chicago.

February 21, 1885
Washington Monument is dedicated.

GROVER CLEVELAND

Democrat, 1885–1889; 1893–1897

Born: March 18, 1837
Died: June 24, 1908
Birthplace: Caldwell, NJ
V.P.: Thomas A Hendricks
First Lady: Frances Folsom

- The Baby Ruth candy bar was named for his daughter Ruth
- Paid someone to fight for him during the Civil War

The only president elected to two non-consecutive terms, Grover Cleveland was a tough and honest man. His willingness to stand up for his principles, however, often hurt his relationship with Congress and the American people.

The son of a Presbyterian minister, young Grover had a strict upbringing that stressed the importance of hard work. In his youth, he worked as a grocery clerk and improved himself by studying law. In the 1860s, he served as assistant district attorney and sheriff in Erie County, New York, before becoming mayor of Buffalo in 1882 and governor of New York between 1883 and 1884.

In 1885, Cleveland became the first Democrat in 24 years to serve as president. Once in office, he helped make the presidency stronger than it had been since the Civil War by re-establishing the president's right to hire and fire government employees without congressional approval. Cleveland also used his veto power liberally, rejecting 2/3 of the bills Congress sent him. His stubborn habits, however, alienated a number of people, and he lost his attempt for re-election in 1888.

Economic depression marked Cleveland's second term in office, and his popularity suffered again. In 1894, when Jacob Coxey and his "army" of angry workers protested the government's failure to create more jobs, Cleveland had Coxey arrested. When a strike at Chicago's Pullman Car Company turned violent that same year, Cleveland became the first president to have the U.S. Army use force against strikers. These actions alienated many American workers, and Cleveland left office an unpopular man.

Cleveland retired to Princeton, New Jersey, where he became a trustee of the local university and occasionally lectured to students. He died in 1908.

Haymarket Square Riot

On May 4, 1886, nearly 1,400 people gathered in Chicago's Haymarket Square to speak out against the excesses of the Gilded Age. Proposing that the United States become a more hospitable place for workers, speakers at this event delivered many passionate speeches that excited the crowd and frightened the police. When close to 200 policemen arrived to break up the gathering, a bomb exploded, killing 7 policemen and wounding many others. This event convinced many Americans that terrorist groups threatened to destroy the U.S. government, and a fearful hysteria swept over the country. Responding to this panic, President Cleveland became less tolerant of labor strikes and other forms of protest.

Immigration

Between 1885 and 1917, nearly 18 million immigrants from Central and Southeastern Europe moved into America's largest cities. Although many of these immigrants could not speak English, they found work in America's numerous factories and helped make the United States a powerful and prosperous nation. Because they often received low wages for hard work, many of these immigrants joined labor unions, making organizations like the American Federation of Labor and the Congress of Industrial Workers stronger than ever.

September 4, 1886
Geronimo, the last Native American chief to surrender, is sent to a Florida reservation.

October 28, 1886
President Cleveland dedicates the Statue of Liberty.

May 15, 1888
The Equal Rights Party meets in Iowa to advance women's rights.

Susan B. Anthony, women's rights advocate

1889

The Great Land Rush

Anxious to settle the American West, the U.S. government opened the Oklahoma Territory to white settlers on April 22, 1889. More than 50,000 people raced to obtain parts of this territory, and, after only a few hours, they had claimed nearly 2 million acres. Earning the nickname "sooners" for their eagerness, these settlers quickly helped develop urban areas, such as Guthrie City and Oklahoma City. Pleased with this process, the U.S. government organized several more settlement drives over the next few years and thereby strengthened its hold on the American frontier.

BENJAMIN HARRISON
Republican, 1889–1893

Born: August 20, 1833
Died: March 13, 1901
Birthplace: North Bend, OH
V.P.: Levi P. Morton
First Lady: Caroline Lavinia Scott

- First president with electricity in the White House
- Called the "Pious Moonlight Dude" for his romantic ways

Benjamin Harrison was a member of one of the most politically distinguished families in American history: his great-grandfather signed the Declaration of Independence, his grandfather served as president, and his father sat in the U.S. Senate. Uninterested in changing the basic structure of American society, Harrison was an inactive president and as a result is often forgotten.

Benjamin Harrison grew up on a 2,000-acre estate with his 8 siblings. As a boy, Harrison was an excellent student, and he graduated from Ohio's Miami University in 1852. After graduation, he moved to Indianapolis, Indiana and became a successful lawyer. In 1860, Harrison was elected to the Indiana Supreme Court.

Determined to make a name for himself, Harrison joined the Union Army in 1862 and fought bravely while serving in General William T. Sherman's Georgia campaign of 1864. After the war, Harrison left the army and in 1881 won a seat in the U.S. Senate. Losing his bid for re-election in 1887, Harrison left the Senate only to win the Republican party's nomination for president one year later.

After narrowly defeating Grover Cleveland in the election of 1888, Harrison proclaimed that the president should be a passive figure. As a result, he let Congress lead the government, asserting himself only in extreme circumstances. However, he helped secure passage of the McKinley Tariff Bill, which protected American businesses from foreign competition. He also allowed Secretary of State James G. Blaine to organize an international conference designed to promote unity within the Western Hemisphere and oversaw the admission of North and South Dakota, Idaho, Montana, Wyoming, and Washington into the United States.

Harrison did not have a temperament suited for the presidency. His desire to be dignified and proper at all times caused others to consider him unfriendly and made it hard for him to work with Congress. Indeed, Harrison's coolness to others caused people to label him "the Human Iceberg." When his wife's health failed during his campaign for re-election in 1892, he lost in interest in the presidency and willingly retired to Indianapolis.

Wounded Knee

On December 29, 1890, 400 American soldiers surrounded 200 Sioux Indians near Wounded Knee Creek, South Dakota. Led by Chief Big Foot and supported by Sitting Bull, these Native Americans had abandoned their government-assigned reservation so they could live according to their own customs. Because this group predicted white people would vanish from the earth, U.S. soldiers considered them dangerous. Thus, when a single warrior failed to surrender his weapon, the American soldiers killed virtually every Sioux, including women and children. The tragedy at Wounded Knee not only ended the Indian Wars, it marked the end of traditional Native American life.

1889

December 6, 1889
Jefferson Davis, the former president of the Confederacy, dies.

June 29, 1890
Henry Cabot Lodge sponsors the Force Bill proposing to protect African Americans seeking the vote.

September 25, 1890
Congress creates Yosemite Park.

January 29, 1896
X-rays are first used to treat breast cancer in the United States.

April 23, 1896
The first moving picture shows in public.

WILLIAM McKINLEY

Republican, 1897–1901

Born: January 29, 1843
Died: September 14, 1901
Birthplace: Niles, OH
V.P.: Garret A. Hobart, Theodore Roosevelt
First Lady: Ida Saxton

- Wife had epileptic seizures
- Told guards not to harm his assassin

A handsome man known for his piercing stare and love of cigars, William McKinley ushered the United States into the age of imperialism. Although McKinley intended to focus on domestic affairs during his presidency, his decision to declare war on Spain and then take control of its former empire made America a recognized world power. McKinley's actions also made the presidency a more powerful office than ever before.

William McKinley was born into a prosperous family involved in the iron-manufacturing business. He briefly attended Pennsylvania's Allegheny College before becoming a country schoolteacher. When the Civil War began, McKinley enlisted in the Union Army as a private and eventually attained the rank of major. After the war, McKinley won a seat in the U.S. House of Representatives and focused on protecting American businesses from foreign competition.

The Republican party's candidate for president in 1896, McKinley sought the support of businessmen while his opponent, William Jennings Bryan, appealed to the interests of farmers and workers. McKinley's conservative message proved more persuasive with American voters, and he easily defeated Bryan.

Once in office, McKinley had to contend with growing turmoil in Cuba. By 1897, Cubans desperately wanted to free themselves from Spanish tyranny. American leaders also wanted to expel Spain from the Western Hemisphere but worried that an independent Cuba would not serve American interests. Determined to defeat Spain and control Cuba, the United States declared war on Spain in 1898 and quickly defeated Spanish forces. McKinley then approved the occupation of Cuba and the annexation of the Philippines, Guam, and Puerto Rico. Although McKinley hoped to uplift the peoples living under American rule, many colonial subjects resented U.S. power and repeatedly rebelled against it.

The War of 1898 made McKinley a popular figure and, with the charismatic Theodore Roosevelt serving as his running mate, he easily won re-election in 1900. In September of 1901, however, Leon Czolgosz, a disgruntled anarchist, shot McKinley in Buffalo, New York. He died 8 days later, becoming America's third president to be assassinated.

The Open Door Policy

In September 1899, the United States attempted to change the way countries practiced foreign affairs. Secretary of State John Hay asked powerful nations to abandon their claims in China and adopt an "open door" policy that allowed all nations to receive equal treatment from the Chinese government. In 1900, England, France, Germany, Russia, Italy, and Japan agreed to respect this policy, and the United States began applying this policy to the rest of the world. Because it leveled the playing field abroad, the open door policy helped the United States become a world power.

Jane Addams (1869–1935)

Concerned that many people—especially immigrants—lived in squalor, Jane Addams became a leader in the American Progressive movement. In 1889, she helped found Hull House in Chicago, Illinois. Staffed by live-in social workers, Hull House offered Chicago's poor hot meals, health care, and educational programs. Hull House employees also worked to make immigrants feel at home in the United States. In 1915, Addams expanded her political vision and founded the International League for Peace and Freedom and served as the chairperson for the International Congress of Women. Although her opposition to American involvement in World War I damaged her reputation, Addams eventually won respect for her love of peace and received the Nobel Peace Prize in 1931.

1896
R. F. Outcault draws the first comic strip, "The Yellow Kid." This strip supplied the name for a dishonest form of news reporting: yellow journalism.

July 1, 1898
Teddy Roosevelt and his troops defeat the Spanish at San Juan Hill.

July 1, 1899
The Gideons begin placing bibles in American hotels.

May 14, 1900
Carrie Nation combats alcohol consumption by destroying Kansas saloons with a hatchet.

THEODORE ROOSEVELT
Republican, 1901–1909

Big Stick Diplomacy

By the time Roosevelt became president, America had emerged as an imperial power. In foreign affairs, Roosevelt's motto was "Speak softly and carry a big stick." This meant combining U.S. diplomacy with displays of military power. In 1907, for example, he ordered the U.S. Navy—known as the Great White Fleet—on a world tour. Three years earlier, he had proclaimed the Roosevelt Corollary to the Monroe Doctrine, reserving for the United States the right to act as an international policeman in Latin America. Following Roosevelt's example, American presidents would become increasingly active in world affairs.

Born: October 27, 1858
Died: January 6, 1919
Birthplace: New York, NY
V.P.: Charles W. Fairbanks
First Lady: Edith Kermit Carow

- Teddy Bears were named for him
- By visiting Panama in 1906, he became the first president to leave the continental United States

Progressivism

Roosevelt formulated his domestic policies in the midst of a broad and diverse reform movement known as Progressivism. In general, Progressives believed that government should play an important role in making society better. Some of the issues Progressives were concerned with included child labor, unsanitary industrial conditions, the conservation of natural resources, and the abuse of power by big businesses. Muckrakers—journalists like Ida Tarbell and Lincoln Steffens who wrote articles exposing corruption in both politics and business—helped rally public support for Progressive causes.

Known as the first modern president, Theodore Roosevelt brought energy, an activist spirit, and unshakable righteousness to the presidency. Crusading with a jutting jaw and pounding fist, he enacted important domestic reforms and pushed a reluctant nation onto the center stage of world affairs.

Roosevelt was born into a wealthy New York family and grew up in an atmosphere of cultured comfort. A sickly, scrawny boy with bad eyesight, he overcame these obstacles to become a good athlete and a lifelong supporter of strenuous exercise. Before he became president, Roosevelt lived an active life, working as a cattle rancher on the Dakota frontier. Although his time in the West was brief, Roosevelt loved being a cowboy. During the Spanish-American War, he commanded a volunteer cavalry unit known as the Rough Riders. Roosevelt emerged from the war a hero and easily won the governorship of New York, arousing audiences with his passion and powerful personality.

Elevated to the presidency after the assassination of McKinley, Roosevelt greatly increased the power of the government to deal with the problems created by a modern industrial society. His domestic policies—called the Square Deal—broke up business monopolies or "trusts," resolved labor strikes, supported land conservation, and regulated the food and drug industries. Abroad, Roosevelt significantly expanded U.S. involvement in world affairs. He believed that strong nations survived and weak ones died, and thus the United States had to struggle with other powerful nations for influence and colonies throughout the world.

When Roosevelt easily won re-election in 1904, he announced that he would not run for president again. Leaving office in 1909, he embarked on an African safari but couldn't resist jumping back into politics. In 1912, he ran for president as the candidate of the Bull Moose (Progressive) party but lost the election. Roosevelt continued to believe in the importance of America's role on the world stage until his death in 1919.

1901

December 1903	1903	1904	1905	January 1906	October 1908
The Wright brothers take flight in a powered glider at Kitty Hawk, N.C.	Pittsburgh defeats Boston in the first World Series.	Construction of the Panama Canal begins.	Einstein publishes theory of relativity, which introduces the equation $E=mc^2$.	Upton Sinclair publishes *The Jungle,* which leads to federal regulation of food and drugs.	Henry Ford introduces the Model T. By 1927, half the cars in the world are Model Ts.

WILLIAM HOWARD TAFT

Republican, 1909–1913

Born: September 15, 1857
Died: March 8, 1930
Birthplace: Cincinnati, OH
V.P.: James S. Sherman
First Lady: Helen Herron

- First president to throw the ceremonial first pitch of the baseball season
- The first president to have a presidential car

Roosevelt's hand-picked successor, William Howard Taft was an effective administrator but a poor politician. He found it difficult to generate enthusiasm for his programs, and he received little credit for his administration's achievements.

Born into a prominent Cincinnati family—his father was President Grant's attorney-general—Taft graduated from Yale University and Cincinnati Law School. He embarked on a successful legal career in Ohio. Taft was not a politician, and his road to the White House ran through administrative posts. In 1900, President McKinley appointed him governor of the Philippines, where he built roads and schools, redistributed land, and gave Filipinos a say in their government. In 1903, Roosevelt made him secretary of war and then endorsed him for president. In 1908, Taft rode Roosevelt's popularity to victory.

As president, Taft promised to continue Roosevelt's popular progressive programs and policies. Unlike Roosevelt, however, Taft did not believe in increasing presidential powers. He was also more conservative by nature. Therefore, although Taft's record on progressive issues such as trust-busting and conservation was generally as good as Roosevelt's, Progressives criticized his policies. At the same time, Taft's economic policies alienated his conservative backers. The result was a divided Republican Party, which helped Democrat Woodrow Wilson win the 1912 presidential election.

Taft, like Roosevelt, wanted to increase U.S. influence abroad. Taft's foreign policy was called "Dollar Diplomacy" because he used financial as well as military might to advance U.S. interests. Taft especially promoted U.S. investments in Latin America, occasionally using force to protect U.S. interests.

Once out of the White House, Taft returned to Yale to teach law. In 1921, he secured his lifelong dream, an appointment as chief justice of the Supreme Court. Although previously cautious in his use of power as president, he used his power as chief justice to enact judicial reform. Taft's years as chief justice were happy ones, and he held the post until his death in 1930.

The Great Migration

Beginning around 1910, thousands of southern blacks moved to northern cities in search of economic opportunity. By 1920, nearly 500,000 African Americans had left the fields of the South for urban centers like New York, Detroit, and Chicago, changing the racial geography of the nation.

The NAACP

In 1909, a group of African-American and white intellectuals formed the National Association for the Advancement of Colored People (NAACP), an organization dedicated to improving conditions for blacks in America. The NAACP, led by the African-American writer and sociologist W. E. B Du Bois, strongly objected to Booker T. Washington's strategy of accommodation and compromise with whites. At the time, Washington was the most influential and admired black in the United States. In 1901, for example, President Roosevelt had invited Washington to dine with him at the White House.

1908
Jack Johnson is first black man to win the world heavyweight boxing championship.

1911
Irving Berlin's "Alexander's Ragtime Band" popularizes ragtime music.

1912
Taft sends U.S. Marines to Nicaragua to crush a rebellion harmful to U.S. business interests.

April 15, 1912
H.M.S *Titanic* sinks on its voyage from England to New York after it hits an iceberg.

1913
States ratify the 16th and 17th Amendments. The 16th makes the income tax constitutional, and the 17th provides for the direct election of senators.

1913

World War I

World War I began as a local European war between Austria-Hungary and Serbia on July 28, 1914. Resulting from the political and economic rivalries caused by the emergence of Germany as a great power, it eventually became a global war involving 32 nations. The Allied Powers, including Great Britain, France, Russia, and eventually the United States, opposed the Central Powers, consisting of Germany, Austria-Hungary, Turkey, and Bulgaria. The majority of the fighting took place in France and consisted of trench warfare, in which each side attacked the other's position but gained little ground. Lasting more than four years, World War I caused nearly 50 million casualties and helped create the conditions that led to World War II.

WOODROW WILSON

Democrat, 1913–1921

Born: December 30, 1856
Died: February 3, 1924
Birthplace: Staunton, VA
V.P.: Thomas R. Marshall
First Ladies: Ellen Louise Axson, Edith Bolling Galt

- Only president to have a Ph.D.
- Only president buried in Washington, D.C.

Driven by a sense of destiny and duty, Thomas Woodrow Wilson pushed a program of domestic reform and asserted U.S. leadership in building a new international order following World War I. Each presidential administration since 1920 has reflected his influence.

The son of a Presbyterian minister, Wilson earned his law degree as well as a doctorate in government and embarked on an academic career. As president of Princeton University, he gained a national reputation as a progressive reformer and in 1910 was elected governor of New Jersey. In the three-way presidential election of 1912, Wilson campaigned successfully on a program called the New Freedom, which stressed breaking up concentrated financial power.

During his first term, Wilson passed many progressive laws, including those reorganizing the U.S. banking system, prohibiting child labor, and giving workers an eight-hour day. This popular legislation carried Wilson to a narrow victory in 1916.

Wilson's second term was dominated by America's entry into World War I. Wilson believed that foreign affairs should be governed by morality and idealism rather than by national interests. By 1917, he had concluded that the U.S. could no longer remain neutral in the European struggle. German submarine attacks on American shipping in particular convinced him of the need to make "the world safe for democracy." America's fresh troops and abundant supplies soon tipped the balance in Europe in favor of the Allies. Wilson personally helped negotiate the Versailles Peace Treaty, which was based on his "Fourteen Points." These points included free trade, self-determination, and an organization for international cooperation called the League of Nations. The Senate, dominated by Republicans, rejected the Versailles Treaty, however.

Despite the warnings of his doctors, Wilson embarked in September 1919 on a national tour to rally public support for the treaty. Exhausted, he suffered a stroke and nearly died. Wilson never recovered fully from his stroke, and for the rest of his term fought in vain for the treaty.

Margaret Sanger (1883–1966)

Trained as a nurse, Margaret Sanger worked in New York City's poor neighborhoods, which convinced her of the widespread need for information about birth control. As a result, Sanger devoted her life to publicizing contraception, even though her actions were illegal at the time. In 1916, she established the first American birth-control clinic in Brooklyn, New York. Sanger went on to found the American Birth Control League (which became Planned Parenthood in 1942), organize the first World Population Conference (1927), and write several books on birth control.

1913
Charlie Chaplin begins his film career and develops his famous "tramp" character.

1913
Exhibition of cubist paintings introduces modern artists like Pablo Picasso to America.

1915
German U-boat sinks the British liner *Lusitania*. Nearly 1,200 passengers drown.

April 1917
U.S. enters World War I.

1919
States ratify the 18th Amendment, banning alcohol and beginning the era of Prohibition.

1920
States ratify the 19th Amendment, giving women the right to vote.

1913

WARREN G. HARDING

Republican,

1921–1923

Born: November 2, 1865
Died: August 2, 1923
Birthplace: Corsica, OH
V.P.: Calvin Coolidge
First Lady: Florence Kling De Wolfe

- First president to visit Alaska
- First president to ride in a car at his inauguration

Warren G. Harding was an easygoing politician who never possessed the leadership or vision required to be an effective president. As a result, the Harding administration is mainly remembered for its corruption, which was revealed after his death.

An influential newspaper publisher in Ohio, Harding used his public speaking ability, friendly personality, and party loyalty to win election to the U.S. Senate in 1914. In 1920, the Republican leadership, meeting in a "smoke-filled room," gave Harding the party's nomination. Heeding the advice of his managers, Harding conducted a front-porch campaign from his home in Ohio, a technique that had been successfully employed by his fellow Ohioans and Republican U.S. presidents Benjamin Harrison and William McKinley. During the campaign, Harding promised that he and the Republican Party could return the United States to "normalcy," a word he invented. By "normalcy," he meant the economic and political isolation that had characterized the United States before it entered World War I. He also meant an end to the government activism and experimentalism of the Progressive movement. This message appealed to Americans weary of idealistic crusades, and Harding won the election in a landslide.

Despite his years in the Senate, Harding found being president difficult. In his domestic and economic policies, he followed a conservative course by slashing taxes, eliminating wartime financial controls, and restricting immigration. In foreign affairs, he oversaw the 1921–22 Washington Naval Conference, which resulted in several disarmament treaties. By 1923, Harding's presidency was unraveling. Persistent rumors about corruption and bribery in his administration, such as the Tea Pot Dome scandal, dominated the headlines. Although there is no proof that Harding himself was corrupt, his good nature and self-indulgent character seem to have blinded him to corruption in his friends and associates. In June 1923, Harding set out on a nationwide speaking tour to assure the American people he was an honest man. Already suffering from poor health, Harding died in San Francisco in August.

The Red Scare

The communist revolution in Russia, postwar strikes, bombings, and riots at home convinced many Americans that anarchy was just around the corner. The government, led by a young J. Edgar Hoover, began raiding radical groups and deporting their members without the benefit of court hearings. Although it began to evaporate by the summer of 1920, the Red Scare led to a wave of nativism and reaction against the modernism of the 1920s. A similar, but more virulent, Red Scare would appear following World War II.

Sacco and Vanzetti

Many Americans believed the 1920s to be a frightening era of change. Defenders of tradition often blamed this change on immigrants and the influence of foreign ideas. The most celebrated criminal case of the time seemed to prove the connection. Two Italian-born anarchists, Nicola Sacco and Bartolomeo Vanzetti, were convicted of robbery and murder in 1920. Although their conviction may have been based on their political ideas and their ethnic origins rather than on evidence of their crimes, the two men went to the electric chair on August 23, 1927.

1920
The Boston Red Sox sell Babe Ruth to the New York Yankees for $125,000.

1920
African-American baseball players form the Negro National League.

1921
The Immigration Restriction Act establishes first quotas on immigration.

1922
T. S. Eliot publishes the poem *The Wasteland*.

1923
More than 500 radio stations are in operation in the United States, fundamentally changing American life.

1923

Mass Culture

During the 1920s, such inventions in communications and transportation as movies, radios, airplanes, and automobiles transformed society. More people than ever before had money to spend and leisure time to fill. Young women especially were eager to exercise new freedoms. Known as "flappers," these independent women sported bobbed hair, smoked cigarettes, wore lipstick, drove cars, and defied general expectations of womanly behavior.

Born: July 4, 1872
Died: January 5, 1933
Birthplace: Plymouth, VT
V.P.: Charlew G. Dawes
First Lady: Grace Anna Goodhue

- His father swore him in as president
- One of three mayors to become president

Harlem Renaissance

After World War I, the neighborhood of Harlem in New York City became a center for an African-American creative outpouring. Black writers, artists, and musicians, such as Langston Hughes and Zora Neale Hurston, described the unique experience of being black in the United States.

CALVIN COOLIDGE
Republican, 1923–1929

A quiet New Englander with a strong sense of public service, Calvin Coolidge served as president during the prosperous and peaceful 1920s. Believing in old-fashioned values, Coolidge was dedicated to preserving the status quo. His homespun personality captivated the nation, and to this day, he remains a symbol of his era.

The son of a Vermont storekeeper, Coolidge graduated from Amherst College, practiced law, and slowly climbed the political ladder in Massachusetts. He rose from city councilman to governor, where he famously broke a Boston policeman's strike by sending in state troops and firing the strikers. Becoming president following Harding's death, Coolidge had to deal with the aftermath of Harding's scandals. His direct, upright manner enabled him to restore confidence in the government in short order. In the 1924 election, "Silent Cal," a symbol of integrity, easily won the presidency by defeating Democratic candidate John W. Davis and Progressive party nominee Robert M. La Follette.

Coolidge's calm style of governing contrasted with the exuberance and extravagance of the Roaring Twenties. He believed that the presidency should revert to its Gilded-Age stance of deference to Congress. He also believed that American prosperity was closely linked to the success of American business. Declaring, "the chief business of America is business," he opposed using government to regulate private enterprise and focused on industrial development at the expense of labor and agriculture. As a result, he supported tax cuts, refused federal aid to farmers, and declined to use government power to check the economic boom. Throughout his term, he viewed with approval the steadily rising stock market and saw no sign of the coming stock market crash. In fact, the president believed the surging prosperity of the time validated his philosophy of governing.

When Coolidge's first full term came to an end in 1929, the country was still thriving, but the president decided not to run for re-election. Coolidge passed his remaining years quietly, writing his autobiography as well as articles advocating individualism and a laissez-faire economic policy. In January 1933, three years into the Great Depression, Coolidge died at his Massachusetts home.

1923

July 1925
John T. Scopes of Dayton, Tennessee, is arrested, tried, and convicted for teaching evolution in school.

1927
The Jazz Singer, the first feature-length talking movie, premieres.

May 21, 1927
Charles Lindbergh lands in Paris, completing the first solo flight across the Atlantic Ocean.

1928
Walt Disney introduces the character Mickey Mouse.

July 24, 1929
The Kellogg-Briand Pact, an agreement making war illegal, goes into effect.

HERBERT HOOVER

Republican, 1929–1933

Born: August 10, 1874
Died: October 20, 1964
Birthplace: West Branch, IA
V.P.: Charles Curtis
First Lady: Lou Henry

- First president born west of the Mississippi River
- Refused to accept a salary for the presidency

Herbert Hoover had established himself as one of America's finest statesman before he became president. Yet when the U.S. economy collapsed during the first stage of his administration, Hoover failed to revitalize the nation's economy and reassure the American people.

Born into a devout Quaker family, Hoover was orphaned at the age of 9 and grew up with his uncle in Oregon. His difficult childhood and religious upbringing caused him to value hard work and mutual self-help. After graduating from Stanford University, he made his fortune as a mining engineer. His work in such places as Australia, China, Russia, and Mexico provided him with an excellent knowledge of world affairs at a young age. When World War I erupted in 1914, Hoover helped evacuate Americans in Europe, officially beginning his career in public service.

During World War I, Hoover headed the Commission for Relief in Belgium and led efforts to ration and distribute food in the United States. When the war ended in 1919, Hoover took charge of the American Relief Administration, which fed and clothed millions of suffering Europeans. Hoover then served as secretary of commerce for Presidents Warren Harding and Calvin Coolidge. In this position, he established himself as a "progressive Republican" by attempting to increase governmental efficiency, boost foreign trade, and promote cooperation between employers and workers.

Elected president in 1928, Hoover planned to work for all Americans by putting "two chickens in every pot and a car in every garage." But the stock market crash of October 1929 ruined his plans. The banking reforms, business loans, and public assistance Hoover sponsored did not restore prosperity. When he allowed the U.S. Army to use force against protesting World War I veterans in 1932, Hoover became even more unpopular. Democrat Franklin D. Roosevelt defeated him easily in that year's election.

After he left the White House, Hoover remained politically active, leading efforts to reorganize the executive branch in 1947 and 1953. Before dying at age 90, he wrote a number of books concerning individual responsibility and good government. His ideas continue to inspire Republican politicians and individual citizens.

The Ashcan School

During Hoover's presidency, artists in New York City's Greenwich Village flourished. Inspired by their surroundings, artists like John Sloan, William Glackens, and Edward Hopper produced paintings celebrating activities that defined urban life. Although a critic named this movement the Ashcan School because he found paintings of slums, tenements, and business districts distasteful, painters like Sloan, Glackens, and Hopper showed that American cities could be as poetic and wondrous as small towns and country villages.

"Black Tuesday"

In October 1929, the U.S. economy began to show signs of weakness. Although financial experts claimed that the economy was fundamentally sound, the stock market collapsed on October 29, known as "Black Tuesday." As businesses across the nation closed their doors, America's wealthiest lost millions of dollars, and common folk lost their jobs. Unemployed people traveled around the country looking for work, living in broken-down settlements called "Hoovervilles" (after the president). Hard times had come to America, and they would not depart for more than 10 years.

1929	**1929**	**1930**	**March 3, 1931**	**August 18, 1931**
Ford introduces the first "station-wagon," a car with a boxy body and extra cargo space.	Elzie Crisler Segar's cartoon character Popeye appears for the first time.	Sinclair Lewis becomes the first American to win the Nobel Prize for Literature.	Hoover designates The Star-Spangled Banner as national anthem.	Japan invades the Chinese province of Manchuria, effectively beginning World War II.

1933

Born: January 30, 1882
Died: April 12, 1945
Birthplace: Hyde Park, NY
V.P.: John N. Garner, Henry A. Wallace, Harry S. Truman
First Lady: Anna Eleanor Roosevelt

- Appointed the first woman, Frances Perkins, to the cabinet
- The only disabled president

The Great Depression

After the stock market crashed in October 1929, Herbert Hoover claimed that prosperity was "just around the corner." The U.S. economy, however, continued to decline, throwing millions of people out of work. When Franklin Roosevelt became president, he experimented with several different reforms. Although the economy gradually improved during Roosevelt's first term, the United States did not regain its economic health until the war in Europe and Asia forced the government to pour massive amounts of money into war-related industries. Defense spending and production created a host of new jobs, provided people with spending money, and set the stage for unprecedented economic growth during the 1940s and 1950s.

FRANKLIN D. ROOSEVELT
Democrat, 1933–1945

The only person to win four presidential elections, Franklin Delano Roosevelt grew to love the presidency. He guided the United States through the Great Depression and World War II, meeting challenges with a unique combination of confidence, vigor, and grace.

Born into an aristocratic New York family, Franklin Roosevelt had an idyllic childhood. An able student, the young FDR attended Massachusetts's Groton Academy and later earned a degree from Harvard University. After college, Roosevelt attended Columbia Law School and practiced law in New York. In 1910, he started his political career by serving in the New York state senate. Three years later President Woodrow Wilson made FDR the assistant secretary of the navy. In 1920, Roosevelt became the Democratic party's vice presidential nominee, but his personality and charm failed to help James Cox win the presidency. In spite of this failure, FDR appeared destined for greatness.

In August 1921, however, tragedy struck Roosevelt when a case of polio left him with only partial use of his legs. Encouraged by his friends and family, Roosevelt refused to abandon politics and became governor of New York in 1928. Roosevelt's illness made him a more compassionate person, and his actions as governor reflected this fact. Between 1928 and 1932, he attempted to help the underprivileged by sponsoring unemployment insurance, child labor laws, and old-age pensions. After promising to make the central government a powerful instrument of reform, FDR won the Democratic party's nomination for president in 1932 and went on to defeat Herbert Hoover in a landslide. Desperate for innovative leadership, America's unemployed citizens hoped that FDR would relieve their suffering.

A whirlwind of activity followed Roosevelt's inauguration. Acting on his promise to offer Americans a "New Deal," FDR created a host of government agencies designed to provide people with both immediate relief and lasting work. Most importantly, the New Deal's National Recovery Administration (NRA), Civilian Conservation Corps (CCC), Public Works Administration (PWA), and Federal Emergency Relief Administration (FERA) restored confidence in the American system of government. Indeed, Roosevelt's New Deal reforms permanently changed the face of American politics by proving that the central government could

1933

February 25, 1933
The first aircraft carrier is launched in Virginia.

May 10–11, 1934
A violent storm blows 300 million tons of topsoil from the Midwest and Southwest, causing a massive migration of farmers to California.

1936
African-American Jesse Owens wins 4 gold medals at the 1936 Olympics in Berlin, disproving Adolph Hitler's theory that Aryan Germans comprise a "master race."

July 2, 1937
Amelia Earhart mysteriously disappears over the Pacific during her proposed flight around the world.

serve as an aggressive source of social and economic change. His wife, Eleanor Roosevelt, helped FDR achieve this lasting change by serving as his conscience. Traveling to impoverished regions that the president did not have the time to visit and meeting with African-American leaders he often chose to ignore, Eleanor made sure the president understood how badly some Americans suffered and how deserving they were of governmental support. Were it not for Eleanor's contributions, President Roosevelt would have made a less effective and less compassionate leader.

Although FDR did not end the Great Depression during his first term, he did ease suffering and easily won re-election in 1936 as a result. During his remaining years in office, international affairs became more important. When war broke out in Europe during 1939, FDR helped transform the U.S. into the "arsenal of democracy" by providing nations like Britain, France, and the Soviet Union with economic and military aid. This

effort proved especially difficult because many congressional leaders did not want to involve the U.S. in the growing global conflict. Yet after the Japanese bombed an American naval base at Pearl Harbor, Hawaii in December 1941, American isolationism evaporated, and FDR brought the U.S. into World War II.

Roosevelt made an excellent war leader. He maintained good relations with Great Britain and the USSR and supervised successful military offensives in Europe and Asia. When he died in April 1945, the U.S. economy was booming again and World War II was almost won. Although many of his actions were imperfect, FDR helped make the U.S. the world's most prosperous and powerful nation. He remains today one of the most respected statesmen in American history.

A. Philip Randolph
(1889-1979)

A pioneer in the civil rights movement, A. Philip Randolph worked to improve the lives of his fellow African Americans. In 1925, Randolph secretly organized the Brotherhood of Sleeping Car Porters, a labor organization that secured decent wages and safe working conditions for African-American railroad workers. In 1940, he helped convince President Roosevelt to form the Fair Employment Practices Committee (FEPC) and thereby provided African Americans with a chance to find jobs in the defense industry. After the war, Randolph worked to desegregate the U.S. armed forces and helped organize the famous "March on Washington" that made civil rights a topic of national concern.

The Second
World War

When a global economic depression struck the world during the 1930s, extremist leaders like Germany's Adolph Hitler, Italy's Benito Mussolini, and Japan's Hideki Tojo came to power. When these men sent armies into neighboring states, world leaders first attempted to appease them before reluctantly preparing for war. World War II officially began when Germany invaded Poland on September 1, 1939, but many American leaders still hoped to shield the United States from this conflict. Deciding that this isolationist policy would not work, President Roosevelt craftily allied the United States with Great Britain, France, and the Soviet Union. When Japan bombed a U.S. naval base at Pearl Harbor, Hawaii, in December 1941, the United States joined the war against Germany, Italy, and Japan, and with the help of its allies, won the war after four years of bitter fighting.

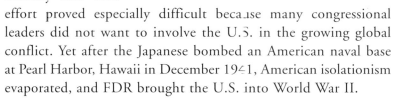

1945

HARRY S. TRUMAN
Democrat, 1945–1953

A feisty man who never shied away from arguments, Harry Truman made a determined and outspoken president. During his time in office, he made the decisions necessary to end World War II, rehabilitate war-torn Europe, and combat communist expansion. In the end, Truman helped make the United States the world's most powerful nation.

A member of a farming family in rural Missouri, the young Truman longed to become a powerful and wealthy man. He consumed the novels of Mark Twain and idolized citizen-soldiers like the Confederacy's Robert E. Lee and ancient Rome's Cincinnatus. Although he did not attend college, Truman benefited from a solid high school education and worked hard to educate himself throughout his life.

When the United States entered World War I, Truman saw combat in France as an artillery captain. He served admirably and, when the war ended, opened a clothing store in Missouri. When the store did not prosper, Truman shut it down in 1922. Although his business failure had left him deeply in debt, Truman decided to abandon his search for wealth in favor of a political career.

After serving as county judge in Missouri, he won a seat in the United States Senate in 1934. As a senator, Truman focused on reforming the American transportation system, eliminating waste in war production, and protecting the interests of small businesses. His colleagues regarded him as a hardworking and honest person.

In 1944, Franklin Roosevelt made Truman his running mate, hoping to benefit from the senator's homespun appeal and solid reputation. Roosevelt soundly defeated Republican Thomas Dewey but died after serving just three months of his new term. Shocked to find himself president, Truman immediately faced a number of difficult decisions. By 1945, World War II had entered its final stages, but Truman feared millions of American soldiers would die invading Japan. He therefore ordered the U.S. military to drop atomic bombs on the Japanese cities of Hiroshima and Nagasaki. After seeing these two cities utterly destroyed, Japan's government quickly surrendered, ending World War II. After the war, Truman moved to restore Europe's economic wellbeing by championing the Marshall Plan, a massive relief effort named after his secretary of state, George C. Marshall.

Born: May 8, 1884
Died: December 26, 1972
Birthplace: Lamar, MO
Party: Democrat
V.P.: Alben W. Barkley
First Lady: Elizabeth Virginia Wallace

- His wife was the longest-living first lady
- Played piano to relax

Levittown

In 1947, William J. Levitt began building a modern American suburb. Located near Island Trees, New York, this settlement--named after Levitt--consisted of 2,000 appealingly affordable and nearly identical homes. Levittown attracted discharged American soldiers who wanted to purchase their own property. Although Levitt only allowed white people to live in his development, the Truman administration provided people with the easy loans they needed to escape city life. People responded in droves and, by 1951, Levittown had become a massive complex of 17,447 homes. For many residents, it symbolized the American dream.

1945

August 6, 1945
The United States drops an atomic bomb on Hiroshima, Japan, destroying the city.

1946
ENIAC, the world's first computer, appears. It revolutionizes the world of technology.

November 6, 1947
America's longest running television program, *Meet the Press*, goes on the air.

1947
Raytheon Company introduces the first microwave oven.

1948
McDonald's, a popular hamburger stand, begins to spread across the United States.

Although Truman hoped to secure good relations with the Soviet Union after the war, he quickly abandoned this effort. As the Cold War dawned in 1946, Truman attempted to maximize American power by forming alliances abroad and using economic and military aid to stop Soviet aggression. In 1947, for example, Truman proclaimed that the United States would assist any nation opposed to communism. Known as the Truman Doctrine, this policy helped prevent the USSR from projecting its power into Greece and Turkey. Furthermore, when the Soviet Union prevented supplies from flowing into western Berlin during the summer of 1948, Truman sponsored the Berlin Airlift. During this 11-month operation, the United States flew supplies into West Berlin around the clock and prevented the city from falling under Soviet control.

Truman also helped to reshape the United States itself after World War II. Hoping to extend FDR's political legacy by offering the American people a "Fair Deal," Truman attempted to raise the minimum wage, expand the Social Security System, offer federal aid to education, and create better housing for the poor. On July 26, 1948, Truman reinforced the growing civil rights movement by ending segregation in the United States armed forces.

After narrowly defeating Republican Thomas Dewey in the election of 1948, Truman experienced a very difficult second term. Although he provided for European military security by supervising the creation of the North Atlantic Treaty Organization (NATO) in 1949, Truman's popularity suffered when China underwent a communist revolution that same year. When Truman chose to fight communist aggression in Korea while supporting one tax increase after another, he became even less popular. Charges of corruption also undermined the president's stature during 1951 and 1952. Although no one accused Truman himself of engaging in unethical behavior, Republicans and Democrats alike believed that he had allowed too many people of questionable character into his administration. When Truman decided to fire an insubordinate General Douglas MacArthur, a World War II hero, from his Korean command, many Americans believed he had gone too far. His popularity sank to an all-time low, and the man from Missouri decided not to seek re-election in 1952. Before leaving the White House, however, Truman campaigned vigorously on behalf of the Democratic party's new nominee, Adlai Stevenson, and reminded friend and foe alike that he retained the spark and fire that had allowed him to guide the nation out of World War II and into the Cold War. Retiring to his home in Independence, Missouri, Truman continued to speak plainly and confidently about world affairs until his death.

The Cold War

Because the United States is a capitalist democracy and the Soviet Union was a communist dictatorship, the two nations naturally distrusted each other. Although the two military giants cooperated during World War II, relations broke down when each attempted to shape the political development of postwar Europe, Asia, and the Middle East. Yet, because the United States and the Soviet Union possessed the ability to destroy each other, they had to avoid direct conflict. In other words, the conflict between the two nations never became "hot," a situation that produced the term Cold War. Lasting more than 40 years, Soviet-American competition produced catastrophic conflicts in places like Korea and Vietnam and caused the American and Soviet governments to distrust their own citizens.

Jackie Robinson

In 1947, Jack Roosevelt Robinson joined the Brooklyn Dodgers and became the first African American to play major league baseball. Before Robinson broke baseball's color barrier, African Americans played in the segregated Negro Leagues and made far less money than their white counterparts. Robinson's spectacular success with the Dodgers proved that African Americans could excel among white athletes and added momentum to America's growing civil rights movement. After Robinson retired from baseball, he became an active member of the National Association for the Advancement of Colored People (NAACP) and, alongside people like Roy Wilkins and Martin Luther King, Jr., worked to end segregation in America.

April 5, 1950
Julius and Ethel Rosenberg are sentenced to death for supplying atomic secrets to the Soviet Union.

June 25, 1950
North Korea invades South Korea and begins the Korean War.

December 29, 1950
African-American Ralph Bunche wins the Nobel Peace Prize.

1950
"Smokey the Bear" becomes a symbol for forest fire prevention.

April 8, 1952
President Truman takes over America's steel mills in order to prevent a national strike.

1953

Rock and Roll

Although people tend to remember the 1950s as a boring era, it was actually a thrilling time. As the U.S. economy boomed, people began having more children than ever before, and those children added a new dimension to American culture. Rock and roll music slowly developed during the early 1950s, as both white and African-American youths injected a new vitality into country music and the blues. Artists like Chuck Berry, Little Richard, and Elvis Presley entertained increasingly large crowds. When musicians appeared on respectable television programs, they became more popular than ever.

Born: October 14, 1890
Died: March 28, 1969
Birthplace: Denison, TX
V.P.: Richard M. Nixon
First Lady: Marie Geneva Doud

- His favorite books were the westerns of Zane Grey
- Considered working as a cowboy in Argentina

McCarthyism

On February 9, 1950, U.S. Senator Joseph McCarthy declared that more than 200 members of the Communist party secretly held positions in the U.S. government. Although McCarthy could not prove that a communist conspiracy to overthrow the U.S. government actually existed, he used televised hearings between April and June of 1954 to ruin the reputations of several innocent people. As time passed, McCarthy's accusations became increasingly wild, and his fellow senators condemned him. Still, McCarthy captured the imaginations of millions of Americans and created an atmosphere of fear and paranoia inside the United States known as "McCarthyism."

DWIGHT D. EISENHOWER
Republican, 1953–1961

A national hero before he entered the White House, Dwight Eisenhower remained incredibly popular throughout his presidency. His economic policies kept the country prosperous, and his grandfatherly presence reassured Americans fearful of nuclear war.

Growing up in a poor but hardworking family in Abilene, Kansas, Eisenhower dreamed of becoming a railroad engineer or a baseball star. After finishing high school, he chose to attend West Point and developed a love for military life. After graduating from West Point in 1915, Eisenhower served in Panama and the Philippines before returning to the U.S. to prepare the army for World War II. On June 6, 1944, Eisenhower led the Allied forces into Europe, and, with the help of the Soviet Union, defeated Germany in 1945. After the war, he served as president of Columbia University and commanded NATO forces in Europe before defeating Democrat Adlai Stevenson in the presidential election of 1952.

As president, Eisenhower first ended the Korean War and then attempted to breathe a spirit of cooperation into American life. His moderate brand of politics focused on reducing government spending, keeping the military strong, and protecting law and order in the U.S. Eisenhower also aggressively opposed the spread of communism abroad and supported the overthrow of potentially pro-Soviet governments in Iran and Guatemala.

Ike's second term proved more difficult than his first. In 1957, African Americans pressed for more civil rights, forcing the reluctant president to have army troops enforce the integration of Little Rock's Central High School. When the Soviet Union launched Sputnik, the world's first space satellite, that same year, Eisenhower had to convince the American people that nuclear war was not imminent. After communists took control of Cuba in 1959 and the Soviet Union shot down an American spy plane in 1960, a dispirited Eisenhower looked forward to retirement. Before leaving office, however, he warned Americans to control the accelerating arms race. The American people still "liked Ike" when he left office.

1953

May 7, 1954
The French fortress falls at Dienbienphu, Vietnam.

May 17, 1954
The Supreme Court decides that segregated facilities are unconstitutional.

April 12, 1955
Jonas Salk announces he has created a cure for polio.

July 17, 1955
Disneyland, a 244-acre amusement park, opens in Anaheim, California.

December 1955
Rosa Parks starts a bus boycott in Montgomery, AL. among the city's African Americans.

May 22, 1959
Benjamin O. Davis, Jr. becomes the first African-American major general.

JOHN F. KENNEDY

Democrat, 1961–1963

Born: May 29, 1917
Died: November 22, 1963
Birthplace: Brookline, MA
V.P.: Lyndon B. Johnson
First Lady: Jacqueline Lee Bouvier

- Favorite meal was tomato soup with sour cream
- Appointed his brother Robert attorney general

The youngest man (and the first Catholic) ever elected president, John F. Kennedy appealed to the idealism of a new generation of Americans. In office for only 1,000 days, he aggressively fought the Cold War abroad and racial injustice at home.

Born into a wealthy and politically active Boston family, John Kennedy possessed a bright mind, robust personality, and movie-star charisma. Returning from World War II a hero, he served in Congress for 14 years. In the 1960 presidential campaign, Kennedy faced the Republican nominee, Vice President Richard Nixon, in four nationally televised debates. Both men spoke well, but Kennedy looked healthy and confident while Nixon looked pale and uncomfortable. When Kennedy won a very close election in 1960, many believed it was because of his performance in the debates.

As president, Kennedy promised to get America moving again with a pragmatic and vigorous program he called the "New Frontier." At home, he took action on poverty and civil rights. Twice, for example, Kennedy sent troops to the South to protect the rights of African-American college students. He also vowed that the United States would land a man on the moon before the end of the decade, and he funded a $5 billion space program to achieve this goal.

Abroad, Kennedy challenged Americans to continue vigorously fighting the Cold War. He created the Peace Corps, an agency that trained American volunteers to perform humanitarian service overseas. He also supported military measures such as the failed invasion of Cuba in 1961. The next year, Kennedy faced a much more serious confrontation with Cuba when U.S. spy planes spotted Soviet nuclear missiles on the island. While the world teetered on the brink of nuclear war, Kennedy used a combination of strength and diplomacy to peacefully resolve the Cuban Missile Crisis. At the same time, however, he increased American involvement in Vietnam.

On November 22, 1963, while riding in an open car in Dallas, Kennedy was assassinated by Lee Harvey Oswald. For millions of shocked Americans, his death symbolized the end of an era of hope and promise.

Civil Rights

During the early 1960s, the grassroots civil rights movement surged ahead in its struggle for African-American equality. In early February 1960, the "sit-in" movement began in Greensboro, North Carolina. In May 1961, a group of "freedom riders" headed for the South on buses to protest segregation. On August 28, 1963, Martin Luther King, Jr. delivered his "I Have a Dream" speech in front of 250,000 people during the March on Washington. For the remainder of the decade, thousands of other activists shared and promoted King's dream.

Berlin Wall

In August 1961, in an effort to prevent East Germans from fleeing to the West, the Soviet-backed government of East Germany built a wall dividing East Berlin from West Berlin. The Berlin Wall remained a powerful symbol of the Cold War until it was torn down in 1989.

1960
Student Non-Violent Coordinating Committee (SNCC) forms to register African-American voters in the South.

April 1961
Soviet cosmonaut Yuri Gagarin becomes the first human to orbit the Earth.

1963
Bob Dylan records "The Times They Are A-Changin'."

1963
Betty Friedan publishes *The Feminine Mystique,* launching a new phase of the women's movement.

1963
Martin Luther King, Jr., writes "Letter from a Birmingham Jail."

1963

LYNDON B. JOHNSON
Democrat, 1963–1969

Born: August 27, 1908
Died: January 22, 1973
Birthplace: Stonewall, TX
V.P.: Hubert H. Humphrey
First Lady: Claudia Alta (Lady Bird) Taylor

- Obsessively watched the evening news on multiple televisions
- Enjoyed high-speed drives around his Texas ranch

Youth Movements

Throughout the 1960s, thousands of young people grew disillusioned with the government and other institutions of authority. By mid-decade, a full-fledged youth revolt had broken out on college campuses across the country. Some rebellious students embraced radical politics, while others—sporting long hair and tie-dyed shirts and taking drugs—joined the counter-culture. Other 1960s movements that fundamentally changed the texture of American life included those for women's, Latino, and gay rights.

As president, Lyndon Johnson displayed a genuine concern for the welfare of the disadvantaged and was committed to the cause of civil rights. Although domestic affairs were his priority, the war in Vietnam ultimately dominated Johnson's presidency. By 1968, the war had eroded the public's faith and confidence in its government and had divided the nation to an extent unparalleled since the Civil War.

A self-made man, Lyndon Johnson worked his way up from a hardscrabble, rural Texas background to become one of the most powerful men in Washington. After serving six terms in the House, he was elected to the Senate in 1948, where he served nearly a decade as the Democratic leader. In the Senate, Johnson was a masterful politician, often resorting to horse-trading and backroom deals to get legislation passed. In 1960, although he wanted the nomination, he agreed to be Kennedy's running mate. Sworn in as president amid the national grief surrounding Kennedy's assassination, Johnson pledged to carry on his predecessor's policies. For example, he signed the Civil Rights Act of 1964, the most far-reaching civil rights measure ever enacted by Congress. In the 1964 election, though possessing none of Kennedy's eloquence or charisma, Johnson won in a landslide and initiated his own domestic program, known as the "Great Society."

Johnson used the momentum provided by his election victory to flood Congress with legislation—more than 200 bills—to achieve economic and social justice. He moved vigorously to pass another landmark piece of civil rights legislation, the Voting Rights Act of 1965. By the end of the year, more than 250,000 African Americans were newly registered to vote. Johnson also declared a government "war on poverty," which included such programs as a Job Corps for inner-city youths and a Head Start program for disadvantaged preschoolers. Other Great Society programs focused on urban renewal, federal aid for schools, and health insurance programs, such as Medicare and Medicaid. Overall, Johnson's Great Society was one of the most extensive reform programs in American history, rivaling the New Deal. Johnson's impressive domestic accomplishments were incompatible with his foreign policy goals, however. America, Johnson soon discovered, could not pay for both the Great Society and the war in Vietnam.

1964
Students at the University of California's Berkeley campus launch the free speech movement.

August 1964
The Gulf of Tonkin Resolution authorizes Johnson to escalate American involvement in Vietnam.

February 1965
The British rock band, The Beatles, excites American youth.

February 1965
Malcolm X is assassinated in New York.

Vietnam

The Vietnam War was the longest, most controversial, and least successful war in U.S. history. Unlike conventional conflicts, the war in Vietnam was largely a guerrilla war—it had no defined front lines. While the United States fought a limited war for limited objectives, the Vietnamese Communists fought an all-out war for national survival. In the end, American support for the war eroded faster than the will of the Vietnamese to continue fighting. Opposition to the war began on American college campuses in 1965. By 1967, anti-war demonstrations in New York and at the Pentagon attracted massive support. The American experience in Vietnam would affect subsequent U.S. policy in the Middle East, Africa, and Latin America.

Johnson inherited the long-standing American commitment to prevent a communist takeover of South Vietnam. Beginning in 1964, he escalated the American role in the Southeast Asian country. By 1967, some half a million U.S. troops were engaged in combat. Despite the increased American effort (including the destructive bombing of North Vietnam), the United States could not achieve a military victory. Each evening, the nightly news announced America's growing casualty figures and made it painfully clear that the Vietnam War was unwinnable. Many Americans began to join the growing anti-war movement and Johnson's popularity declined. By 1968, the president was avoiding public appearances because of anti-war demonstrations, and several candidates were vying for the Democratic nomination. Still, it came as a shock when on March 31, 1968, Johnson announced on national television that he would not seek another term as president. Disillusioned and frustrated by the war, Johnson retired to Texas to write his memoirs. Entitled *The Vantage Point* it explained Johnson's disillusionment with Vietnam and his regrets about not achieving a truly "great society." He died in 1973, two years before the last American soldiers left Vietnam.

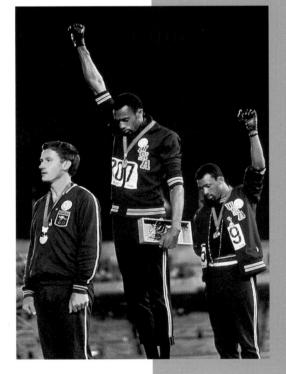

Black Power

In the midst of its legislative success during the mid-1960s, the civil rights movement began to fragment. The separatist and militant philosophy of "black power," advocated by black leaders like Malcolm X and Stokely Carmichael, challenged Martin Luther King's program of nonviolent protest. Widely publicized and highly visible, the black power movement focused needed attention on the plight of poor, inner-city African Americans.

August 11–16, 1965
Watts, a predominantly poor black community in Los Angeles, explodes in riots and looting.

September 1966
Star Trek debuts on NBC.

1966
Jimi Hendrix popularizes the electric guitar.

January 30, 1968
The North Vietnamese Army and its allies in the South launch the Tet Offensive, a massive surprise attack on cities in South Vietnam.

April 4, 1968
James Earl Ray assassinates Martin Luther King, Jr.

1969

47

Roe v. Wade

During the late 1960s, abortion became a controversial political issue. In 1973, the Supreme Court, in *Roe v. Wade,* ruled that women had a legal right to an abortion during the first three months of pregnancy. "Pro-life" forces widely criticized the decision and have worked vigorously since then to overturn it. "Pro-choice" advocates, in contrast, praised it and have fought just as vigorously for a woman's right to choose whether or not to have an abortion. Today, the issue of abortion continues to provoke heated debate.

Born: January 9, 1913
Died: April 22, 1994
Birthplace: Yorba Linda, CA
V.P.: Spiro T. Agnew, Gerald R. Ford
First Lady: Thelma Catherine (Pat) Ryan

- The first president to have visited all fifty states
- Suffered from insomnia during his presidency

Woodstock

One of the most memorable events of the 1960s was the Woodstock Music Festival, held in upstate New York in August 1969. Some 500,000 young people showed up to listen to Jimi Hendrix, Joan Baez, Jefferson Airplane, and many other performers. For three days the crowd reveled in good music, cheap drugs, and free love. Woodstock's good vibes were short-lived, however. When promoters tried to repeat the scene four months later at Altamont, California, violence ensued and four spectators were killed.

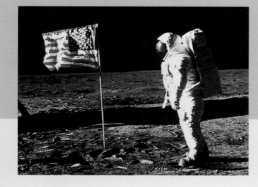

RICHARD M. NIXON
Republican, 1969–1974

Richard Nixon faced an America troubled by urban violence and deeply divided by the Vietnam War. Ultimately, Nixon's actions and personality served to heighten rather than reduce the tensions in American society.

Born in suburban Los Angeles, Nixon grew up in a working-class Quaker family. In 1946, having completed law school and a wartime stint in the navy, Nixon jumped into the political arena. As a congressman and a senator, he rapidly rose through the Republican ranks by manipulating and feeding anti-communist hysteria. He served two terms as Eisenhower's vice president but lost the 1960 election to John F. Kennedy. In the 1968 contest, Nixon eked out a narrow victory, promising an honorable peace in Vietnam and harmony at home.

Despite Nixon's campaign pledge, the American withdrawal from Vietnam was slow and not very honorable. Faced with daily and increasingly violent anti-war demonstrations, Nixon gradually reduced the number of American combat troops. At the same time, he expanded the intensity and scope of the bombing campaign. By the time a settlement was finally reached in 1973, another 20,000 Americans had died and countless more Southeast Asians had been killed or wounded. Nixon, working with Secretary of State Henry Kissinger, was more successful in other areas of foreign policy. For example, he fundamentally shifted the pattern of the Cold War by pursuing détente, a policy of improved relations with China and the Soviet Union.

Nixon easily won re-election in 1972, but the Watergate crisis soon destroyed his presidency. The scandal stemmed from the Nixon administration's involvement in and cover-up of a burglary at the Democratic National Committee offices in the Watergate apartment complex. Watergate was a serious constitutional crisis and part of a larger pattern of criminal behavior sanctioned by the Nixon White House. Faced with certain impeachment, Nixon resigned from office in August 1974, the only president ever to do so. In retirement, Nixon wrote and traveled widely and gradually regained some public respect, especially as a foreign policy expert.

July 21, 1969
Astronaut Neil Armstrong is the first man to walk on the moon.

April 22, 1970
Environmentalists organize the first Earth Day.

May 4, 1970
The members of the Ohio National Guard kill four students at Kent State University.

February 1972
Nixon visits the People's Republic of China.

May 1972
The United States and the Soviet Union sign a nuclear arms control agreement known as SALT.

GERALD R. FORD

Republican, 1974–1977

Born: July 14, 1913
Birthplace: Omaha, NE
V.P.: Nelson A. Rockefeller
First Lady: Elizabeth Anne (Betty) Bloomer Warren

- Teased by comedians because of his famous clumsiness
- Had the Marine Corps Band play the University of Michigan fight song instead of Hail to the Chief

Known for his warmth and integrity, Gerald Ford reassured a nation weary of political scandal. He inherited an economy suffering from inflated prices and high unemployment but worked diligently to restore prosperity.

Born with the name Leslie Lynch King, Jr., Ford took the name of his stepfather when his mother remarried in 1916. A strapping lad, Ford attended the University of Michigan and became a star football player. After graduating in 1935, Ford attended Yale Law School while coaching the university's football team. During World War II, he joined the navy, serving in the South Pacific and rising to the rank of lieutenant commander. When the war ended, Ford practiced law in Michigan before winning a seat in the U.S. House of Representatives in 1948. He served in the House for 25 years, acting as the Republican party's minority leader between 1965 and 1973. He then became vice president after his predecessor, Spiro T. Agnew, resigned in disgrace, and became president after the Watergate scandal forced Richard Nixon from office.

As president, Ford issued Nixon a full pardon, making it impossible to prosecute the former president. Although Ford hoped pardoning Nixon would allow the country to heal itself, the American people continued to distrust their government. Ford's efforts to revive the nation's slumping economy also failed to inspire the people.

Ford also faced a number of challenges abroad. Hoping to secure peace in the Middle East, Ford and Secretary of State Henry Kissinger helped settle the Israeli-Arab War of 1973. In addition, when the government of South Vietnam began collapsing in April 1975, Ford supervised the final evacuation of Americans from the region. Less than one month later, Ford ordered the rescue of the *Mayaguez*, a U.S. cargo ship that Cambodia's government had captured.

Before Ford lost a hotly contested election to Democrat Jimmy Carter in 1976, his honesty helped restore confidence in the American political system. He remains the only man to serve as vice president and president without being elected to either office.

Human Rights

During the first half of the 1970s, leaders of both the Soviet Union and the United States worked to improve relations between their countries. One outgrowth of this effort was the Helsinki Final Act of 1975, an agreement that bound the United States, the Soviet Union, and European nations to respect human rights. This agreement made it easier for discontented groups inside these nations to criticize their governments without fearing punishment. In fact, the Final Act nurtured a generation of reformers inside the Soviet empire who helped end the Cold War and ensured the collapse of the Soviet Union itself.

Gloria Steinem (1934–)

A gifted writer capable of reaching a large audience, Gloria Steinem became a leading feminist during the 1970s. She entered the working world as a journalist, writing for such magazines as *Vogue, Glamour,* and *Cosmopolitan.* Later, her articles for *New York Magazine* brought a woman's view of the American political process to public attention. In 1971, Steinem worked with fellow feminists Betty Friedan, Bella Abzug, and Shirley Chisolm to form the National Women's Political Caucus and, later that year, helped produce the first issue of *Ms.,* a feminist magazine. Consistently arguing that women should have equal employment and educational opportunities, Steinem made sure women had a greater voice in American politics.

September 8, 1974
President Ford pardons Richard Nixon for Watergate.

1974
Hank Aaron breaks Babe Ruth's homerun record.

July 17, 1975
American and Soviet spacecraft link, reinforcing the policy of détente.

1975
International Women's Year is observed around the world.

July 4, 1976
America celebrates its bicentennial.

1977

The Hostage Crisis

When Muslim revolutionaries took control of Iran in 1978, Iranian-American relations suffered. Determined to show their contempt for the United States, 500 Iranian students stormed the U.S. embassy on November 4, 1979 and captured 66 Americans. Although the U.S. government negotiated on behalf of the hostages, the Iranian government refused to relinquish their American captives. When a military rescue attempt failed on April 24, 1980, frustrated Americans decorated their homes with yellow ribbons to honor the hostages. On January 20, 1981, Iran finally agreed to release the hostages after holding them for 444 days.

JAMES E. CARTER

Democrat, 1977–1981

Jimmy Carter planned to make government more efficient and compassionate. A vocal champion of human rights during his time in office, he has continued to fight for the disadvantaged as a private citizen.

Carter grew up on his family's Georgia peanut farm before attending the U.S. Naval Academy. After graduating with high marks in 1946, Carter served in the navy for seven years. He then returned to the peanut farming business before becoming a Georgia state senator in 1963 and governor of the state in 1970. As governor, Carter stressed the importance of ecological conservation and governmental efficiency.

In 1976, Carter won the Democratic party's nomination for president and narrowly defeated Gerald Ford in the general election. As president, Carter reformed the civil service, expanded the national park system, and created the Department of Education. He also pardoned nearly 10,000 Americans guilty of evading the draft during the Vietnam War. Carter, however, did not establish good relations with Congress and, as a result, could not cope with the nation's energy crisis.

Carter's greatest successes came in 1978, when he helped Israel's Prime Minister Menachem Begin and Egyptian leader Anwar al-Sadat end a long-standing state of war between their two nations. Carter also negotiated a nuclear arms limitation treaty with the Soviet Union, but the U.S. Senate did not ratify the agreement because the Soviet Union invaded Afghanistan in 1979. That same year Carter faced an even greater problem when revolutionary Iranian students stormed the American embassy in Tehran, Iran, and took 66 hostages. Although Carter worked hard to secure their release, the hostages remained in Iran for 14 months, going free on Carter's last day in office.

Carter's inability to work with Congress or free the hostages hurt his popularity, and he lost his bid for re-election in 1980. As a private citizen, Carter volunteered with Habitat for Humanity, an organization that builds homes for needy people around the world. In addition, he has written several books and spoken on behalf of world peace and human rights.

Born: October 1, 1924
Birthplace: Plains, GA
V.P.: Walter F. Mondale
First Lady: Eleanor Rosalyn Smith

- Studied nuclear physics while at the Naval Academy
- First elected president since 1932 not to win a second time

Space Exploration

Although the 1970s are not remembered as a time of exploration, the U.S. space program produced a great deal of new information about the Earth's solar system during these years. In December 1978, two unmanned American spacecraft, Pioneer I and Pioneer II, reached Venus and provided scientists with new information about the planet's atmosphere and surface. Only three months later, another U.S. vessel, Voyager I, broadcast back to the United States detailed pictures of Jupiter's surface and moons. And in September 1979, Pioneer II passed within 13,000 miles of Saturn, discovering a new moon and additional rings surrounding the planet.

1977

August 12, 1977
The first space shuttle completes a test flight.

March 26, 1979
In a ceremony held in Washington, D.C., Egypt's Anwar al-Sadat and Israel's Menachem Begin sign a peace treaty ending a formal state of war that had existed between the two states since 1948.

May 18, 1980
Washington state's Mount St. Helens erupts with the force of 500 atomic bombs.

Summer 1980
The U.S. boycotts the Olympics to protest the Soviet Union's invasion of Afghanistan.

RONALD REAGAN

Republican, 1981–1989

Born: February 6, 1911
Died: June 5, 2004
Birthplace: Tampico, IL
V.P.: George Bush
First Lady: Nancy Davis

- At 69, the oldest person ever elected president
- Submitted the first trillion-dollar budget to Congress

Known as "the great communicator," Ronald Reagan practiced a conservative brand of politics. He attempted to reduce the size of the central government while increasing America's military strength.

Always drawn to the spotlight, Reagan played football and acted in school plays while attending Illinois's Eureka College. After graduation, he became a radio sports announcer and, in 1937, moved to Hollywood to make movies. During the 1950s Reagan developed strong anti-communist beliefs and took an interest in politics. He became governor of California in 1966 and served two terms. Reagan remained an active member of the Republican party throughout the 1970s and won the party's nomination for president in 1980.

After defeating Jimmy Carter in the election of 1980, Reagan focused on cutting taxes, reducing inflation, and strengthening the military. Reagan believed that these policies would revive the national economy and allow the average citizen to live more comfortably. Although his programs drastically increased the national debt, the economy gradually improved and paved the way for Reagan's re-election in 1984.

During his second term, Reagan worked with Soviet leader Mikhail Gorbachev to improve Soviet-American relations. In 1987 and 1988, Reagan and Gorbachev agreed to reduce the number of Soviet and American nuclear missiles. Reagan, however, remained strongly opposed to the spread of communism abroad and worked hard to undermine governments in Central America, Africa, and Asia as a result. His administration's attempt to defy Congress and topple Nicaragua's government produced a long investigation that stained the reputation of many high-level government officials. Investigators of the Iran-Contra scandal, however, never discovered Reagan's role in this illegal operation, and he remained popular when he left the White House in 1989.

After retiring, Reagan continued to support conservative politics before falling prey to Alzheimer's disease, a degenerative brain disorder. An American icon, Reagan remains an inspirational figure. His ideas continue to enliven political debates.

The Reagan Revolution

Ronald Reagan's plan to rebuild American strength by reducing taxes and fortifying the military inspired a generation of conservative citizens. These basic ideas remained alive after he left office, influencing the thinking of people both inside and outside of government. When the Republican party won a series of smashing victories in the congressional elections of 1994, many of the winning candidates considered themselves the political offspring of Reagan and based their policies on his ideas.

Glasnost

When the Soviet Union invaded Afghanistan in 1979, Soviet-American relations suffered. President Reagan promised to oppose Soviet aggression during the election of 1980 and referred to the Soviet Union as an "evil empire" after taking office. When Mikhail Gorbachev became leader of the Soviet Union in March 1985, however, Cold War tensions began to

relax. Pursuing a policy of Glasnost, or "openness," Gorbachev worked with Reagan to reduce the risk of nuclear war and to increase cultural and technological exchanges between the United States and the Soviet Union. By the time Reagan left office in 1988, the end of the Cold War was in sight.

September 21, 1981
Sandra Day O'Connor becomes the first female member of the U.S. Supreme Court.

1984
Geraldine Ferraro becomes the first female candidate for vice president.

January 28, 1986
The space shuttle *Challenger* explodes 1 minute after taking off, killing all the astronauts, including a schoolteacher.

1987
Toni Morrison publishes *Beloved*, and wins the Pulitzer Prize one year later.

1989

The Persian Gulf War

Determined to make Iraq the Middle East's dominant power, Saddam Hussein commanded the Iraqi army to invade Kuwait, a small, oil-rich nation, in August of 1990. President Bush considered Iraq's action an example of "naked aggression" and vowed to expel Iraqi forces from Kuwait. Known as "Operation Desert Storm," this offensive used a combination of sea, air, and land forces to overwhelm the Iraqi military in just over 100 hours. Saddam Hussein, however, remained in power after the war and continued to menace American interests in the Middle East.

GEORGE H. W. BUSH
Republican, 1989–1993

A distinguished World War II veteran with a long career in public service, George H. W. Bush hoped his moderate brand of politics would keep America strong and prosperous. He was the first president to direct U.S. foreign policy after the Cold War.

Growing up in a world of comfort and privilege, Bush learned to appreciate the concept of public service early in life. He became

Born: June 12, 1924
Birthplace: Milton, MA
V.P.: J. Danforth Quayle
First Lady: Barbara Pierce

- The first incumbent vice president elected since Martin Van Buren
- The first president to have been director of the Central Intelligence Agency

a student leader while attending Phillips Academy but postponed college to serve in World War II. Becoming the youngest pilot in the U.S. Navy, Bush flew 58 combat missions against the Japanese and won the Distinguished Flying Cross for bravery. After the war, Bush attended Yale University, graduating with an economics degree in 1948.

After college, Bush moved to western Texas and made his fortune in the oil business. In 1966, he was elected to the U.S. House of Representatives and served two terms as a moderate, pro-business Republican. Bush then served as ambassador to the United Nations, Chairman of the Republican National Committee, U.S. envoy to China, and director of the Central Intelligence Agency. He sought the Republican nomination for president in 1980 and chose to become Ronald Reagan's vice president when his own campaign failed.

In 1988, Bush won the presidency, promising to make the United States a "kinder, gentler nation." During his term, Bush treated the fallen Soviet empire with caution and organized the overthrow of Panama's corrupt leader, Manuel Noriega. In January 1991, Bush supervised "Operation Desert Storm," a U.S.-led United Nations offensive that expelled Iraq's armed forces from Kuwait. But Bush's domestic policies were less successful. Because the government spent more money than it earned, the U.S. economy began to slump in the early 1990s. Bush's decision to raise taxes alienated conservative Republicans, and many other voters began to doubt his ability to restore prosperity.

While running for re-election in 1992, Bush seemed unwilling to wage a vigorous campaign and paid for his reluctance. In contrast to the dynamic and personable Bill Clinton, Bush appeared cold and remote to many voters and lost the 1992 election as a result. In retirement, he has promoted the political careers of his sons, Jeb and George W.

The L.A. Riots

When an all-white jury acquitted four policemen of beating an African-American citizen named Rodney King in April 1992, riots broke out in the predominantly African-American and Latino areas of Los Angeles, California. Jurors claimed that the policemen were just doing their jobs when they violently subdued King, but many minorities believed King's beating grew out of lingering racial prejudice in the United States. The rioting lasted several days, causing President Bush to use the military to restore order in Los Angeles.

June 21, 1989
A Supreme Court ruling allows the burning of American flags.

March 13, 1991
The Exxon Corporation agrees to pay $900 million in damages for spilling massive amounts of oil in Alaska's Prince William Sound.

October 15, 1991
Clarence Thomas becomes second African American to sit on the U.S. Supreme Court.

November 7, 1991
Basketball star Earvin "Magic" Johnson announces that he is HIV-positive.

WILLIAM J. CLINTON

Democrat, 1993–2001

Born: August 19, 1946
Birthplace: Hope, AR
V.P.: Albert Gore Jr.
First Lady: Hillary Rodham

- Plays the saxophone
- In 1969, he integrated a whites-only swimming pool in Hot Springs, Arkansas

The first president born after World War II, Bill Clinton moved his party closer to the political center. During his eight years in office, he faced questions about his personal character and engaged in bruising battles with Republicans in Congress.

When Bill Clinton was in high school, he met President Kennedy and was inspired to enter politics. A graduate of Georgetown University, Clinton won a Rhodes scholarship to Oxford and then earned a law degree from Yale. At age 32, he was elected governor of his native Arkansas. Serving three terms as governor, he emerged as a dynamic leader. Stressing economic issues, Clinton won the 1992 presidential election despite controversial allegations of adultery and avoiding the draft during the Vietnam War.

As president, Clinton appointed more women and minorities to his cabinet than had any previous president. During his first term, Clinton focused on legislation to increase foreign trade and to address social issues, such as health care, education, welfare reform, and gun control. He successfully lobbied for agreements that lowered trade barriers but found passing social legislation more difficult. Extensive health-care reform efforts, for example, never made it through Congress. Following the Republican 1994 Republican congressional victories, Clinton's relationship with Congress became even more strained, resulting in two partial government shutdowns.

Since before his election in 1992, Clinton had faced allegations of both financial and sexual scandal. Investigation of his early business dealings in Arkansas, dubbed the "Whitewater Affair," continued after Clinton won re-election in 1996. In the course of this and related inquiries, it surfaced that the president had an affair with a White House intern and lied about it. Although public reaction to the scandal was mixed, the Republican-controlled Congress impeached the president in January 1999. Clinton survived his trial in the Senate and, ever responsive to changing public moods, remained popular. During his remaining time in office, the president worked to secure his legacy by maintaining America's record economic growth and traveling abroad to mediate international disputes.

Foreign Policy Challenges

Facing a complex international situation, the Clinton administration struggled to find a consistent foreign policy vision. Emphasizing Wilsonian themes of democracy and humanitarian intervention, Clinton used force to try to settle bloody conflicts in Rwanda, Somalia, Haiti, and the volatile states of the former Yugoslavia. These efforts had mixed results. Clinton had more success in the Middle East, overseeing several agreements between Israel and the Palestine Liberation Organization (PLO). Despite several interruptions, the American-sponsored Middle East peace process continues.

Anti-Government Sentiment

A burgeoning "militia" movement spread across the country in the 1990s. Convinced that the government was conspiring against individual liberties (especially the right to bear arms), these extremist organizations challenged federal authority. Militia membership swelled in reaction to deadly confrontations between the government and separatist groups at Ruby Ridge, Idaho, and Waco, Texas. On April 19, 1995, the second anniversary of the Waco incident, a massive truck bomb exploded in front of a federal office building in Oklahoma City, Oklahoma, killing 168 people and wounding 600 others. The Oklahoma City bombing shocked and saddened the nation. It also revealed the depth of the paranoid strain of American politics and society.

April 1995
Republicans' "Contract with America," focuses on basic questions of government philosophy.

January 1997
Madeleine K. Albright, a veteran diplomat, becomes the first female secretary of state.

June 1998
After winning his sixth NBA title, Michael Jordan retires from basketball.

April 20, 1999
Colorado teens shock the nation by killing several Columbine High classmates.

January 1, 2000
Fears of a global computer failure—known as the Y2K bug—prove groundless.

2001

September 11, 2001

On September 11, 2001, terrorists from the Al Qaeda organization hijacked four airplanes and crashed them into the two World Trade Center towers in New York City, the Pentagon in Washington, D.C., and a field in western Pennsylvania, killing nearly 3,000 people. The attacks left Americans and people around the world stunned and saddened. After the shock subsided, a wave of sympathy and patriotism swept the nation, as support poured in for the survivors and victims' families. Images and stories from September 11—including the courage and heroism displayed by firefighters, police officers, and other rescue workers—remain powerful reminders of sacrifice and the value of public service.

GEORGE W. BUSH
Republican, 2001–

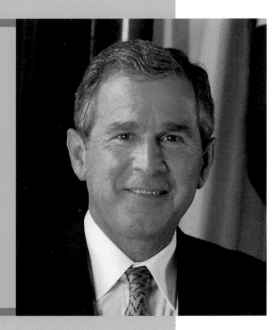

Born: July 6, 1946
Birthplace: New Haven, CT
V.P.: Richard Cheney
First Lady: Laura Welch

- Appointed retired General Colin Powell as the first African-American Secretary of State.
- The first president to raise more than $200 million for his re-election campaign.

Only the second president's son to win the White House himself, George W. Bush won one of the closest elections in American history. The course of his first term—as well as that of the nation—was forever changed by the terrorist attacks of September 11, 2001.

Born into a distinguished political family, George W. Bush grew up in Texas before attending Yale University. After graduating in 1968, Bush trained as a fighter pilot in the Texas Air National Guard. He then earned a masters degree from Harvard University and returned to Texas, where he worked in the oil industry and became part owner of Major League Baseball's Texas Rangers. Bush later served as governor of Texas for six years, cutting taxes and focusing on educational and welfare reform. Hoping to follow in his father's presidential footsteps, he captured the Republican nomination in 2000, but the election was a long and contentious one. After a month of recounts and uncertainty, Bush won the electoral vote and the presidency.

Domestic issues like reducing taxes and improving education dominated Bush's first eight months in office. But it was events of September 11, 2001, that shaped the remainder of his first term. Bush immediately reassured the American people that the government was working to keep them safe, declaring a global war on terrorism. Under his direction, U.S. forces invaded Afghanistan, which had given support to terrorists. Back at home, Bush created the Department of Homeland Security to protect America against further attacks. He also had the difficult task of finding the proper balance between national security and civil liberties.

In March 2003, Bush argued that it was necessary to attack Saddam Hussein's Iraq as part of the war on terrorism. Many foreign powers and everyday Americans protested Bush's decision to invade the country because they did not believe it posed an urgent threat to America. The U.S. military liberated the Iraqi people, and, despite the controversies surrounding the war, George W. Bush won re-election by convincing Americans that he was best equipped to wage the war on terrorism, as well as improve health care, schools, and the economy.

Education

Fulfilling a campaign promise to reform the American education system, George Bush worked successfully with Congress to pass the No Child Left Behind Act (NCLB). This plan to improve the nation's schools instituted the most sweeping changes to public education in a generation. A blend of new requirements, new incentives, and new funding, NCLB expanded the federal government's role in education to ensure that children in every public school classroom benefited from well-prepared teachers and safe learning environments.

January 2001
Hillary Clinton joins the Senate as the first First Lady to be elected to a public office.

September–October 2001
Letters containing deadly anthrax spores are mailed to government and media offices, killing five people and sickening seventeen.

March 24, 2002
Halle Berry becomes the first African-American to win the Academy Award for Best Actress.

October 7, 2003
Actor Arnold Schwarzenegger wins the highly publicized California recall election to become governor.

Glossary of Terms

ABOLITIONISM: A political movement dedicated to making slavery illegal throughout the United States.

AMBASSADOR: A person appointed to represent governments in foreign countries.

AMENDMENT: An addition to the Constitution requiring the approval of Congress and 3/4 of the states.

ANNEXATION: An incorporation or absorption of a country or territory into an existing nation.

APPEASEMENT: A policy based on compromising with potential enemies in order to secure peace.

ARMS RACE: A competition between states involving the production and stockpiling of weapons.

CABINET: A group of people chosen by the presidents to advise them on issues.

CAPITALISM: An economic system in which private individuals, not government, control business.

COMMUNISM: An economic system in which government, not private individuals, control business.

DELEGATE: A person who represents states at political conventions.

DEMOCRACY: A political system in which people vote for their own leaders.

DRAFT: A system in which the government requires people to serve in the military.

EMANCIPATION: A condition in which people are legally free.

EXPANSIONISM: A movement concerned with increasing a country's physical size.

FEMINISM: A political movement dedicated to the advancement and protection of women's rights.

IMPEACHMENT: The process by which Congress votes to remove the president or his appointees from office.

IMPERIALISM: A system in which stronger states have political and economical control over weaker ones.

ISOLATIONISM: A philosophy encouraging governments to restrict contact with foreign countries.

INTEGRATION: A political movement designed to promote cooperation between racial groups.

NULLIFICATION: A philosophy arguing that state and local governments can ignore or overturn the laws of the central government.

REVOLUTION: A political process in which people overthrow existing rulers.

SECESSION: A political act in which states break their bonds with the central government.

SECTIONALISM: A political philosophy that emphasizes regional differences.

SEGREGATION: A system of laws and customs designed to isolate and oppress minority groups.

TRUST: A group of big businesses that cooperate with each other in order to maximize their profits.